After the Gods

Steve Waters' first play for the Hampstead Theatre, *English Journeys*, was produced as part of the first New Directions Series in 1998. He was subsequently appointed Pearson Writer-in-Residence at Hampstead. He has translated Philippe Minyana's play *Habitats* for the National Theatre Studio, written a one-act play, *London Bridge*, for Paines Plough Wild Lunch IV Season and performed at the Bridewell Theatre, London, in 2000, and *The Diagnosis* for RNT Education and Y-Touring, which received a reading in the Cottesloe. In addition he has written two plays for East Anglian theatre companies: *Flint People* for Tiebreak (2000) and *The Cull* (2001) for Menagerie. He also writes for television (*Safe House*, BBC, 2001) and radio (*The Moderniser*, Radio 4 2001). Steve has also been Judith E. Wilson Junior Fellow at the University of Cambridge and currently lectures in Drama for the Education Faculty there.

STEVE WATERS

After the Gods

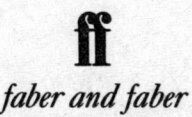

faber and faber

First published in 2002
by Faber and Faber Limited
3 Queen Square, London WC1N 3AU

Typeset by Country Setting, Kingsdown, Kent CT14 8ES
Printed in England by Mackays of Chatham plc, Chatham, Kent

All rights reserved

Copyright © Steve Waters, 2002

Steve Waters is hereby identified as author
of this work in accordance with Section 77 of the
Copyright, Designs and Patents Act 1988

All rights whatsoever in this work, amateur or professional,
are strictly reserved. Applications for permission
for any use whatsoever including performance rights
must be made in advance, prior to any such proposed use,
to Micheline Steinberg Playwrights, 409 Triumph House,
187–191 Regent Street, London W1R 7WF. No performance
may be given unless a licence has first been obtained

*This book is sold subject to the condition that it shall not, by
way of trade or otherwise, be lent, resold, hired out or otherwise
circulated without the publisher's prior consent in any form of
binding or cover other than that in which it is published and
without a similar condition including this condition being
imposed on the subsequent purchaser*

A CIP record for this book
is available from the British Library

ISBN 0–571–21596–3

**To Hero and Joseph
and in memory of Fred Meek**

We are not free
and the sky can still fall on our heads

Antonin Artaud

After the Gods was first performed at the Hampstead Theatre, London, on 12 June 2002. The cast was as follows:

Michel Beaudricourt Fred Pearson
Marie Beaudricourt Susan Engel
Kate Leverhulme Katie Blake
Fergus O'Connor Conor Mullen
Dale Stillman Joseph Mydell
Sandilya Pandit Amita Dhiri
Gwynn Thomas Gabrielle Lloyd
Stephen Fulton Tom Smith

Director Gemma Bodinetz
Set and Costume Designer Liz Ascroft
Lighting Designer Richard G. Jones
Sound Designer John A. Leonard

Characters

Michel Beaudricourt
French cultural commentator, sixty-five

Marie Beaudricourt
his wife, seventy

Kate Leverhulme
translator, twenty-five

Fergus O'Connor
Irish academic, thirty-eight

Dale Stillman
American poet, forty

Sandilya Pandit
academic, thirty-two

Gwynn Thomas
academic, forty-five

Stephen Fulton
academic, thirty-two

Setting

Act One: two hotel rooms, Fergus and Dale's flat in Aberystwyth, three rail-station waiting rooms, at various times through the early hours of a morning.

Act Two: University of Aberystwyth campus.

Act Three: the same, a lecture hall.

Act Four: Aberystwyth shoreline.

Time

The present. Spring.

AFTER THE GODS

Act One

The following scenes and settings appear simultaneously onstage:

  Beaudricourt / Marie / Kate in a hotel room;
  Fergus / Dale in bedroom;
  Sandy / Gwynn in various rail stations;
  Stephen Fulton in a hotel room.

We are aware of the presence of all characters throughout the act.
  Beaudricourt and Kate standing, Marie on bed, asleep.

Beaudricourt She sleeps.

Kate She must be tired.

Beaudricourt She's older.

They look at each other. He kisses her.

Kate I don't want to . . . with her here.

Beaudricourt You have given me my life again.

He kisses her more energetically, she breaks away.

Kate We need to finish this. I think the opening's problematic.

Beaudricourt Read it back to me.

Kate 'We fuck Hamlet behind the arras, we fuck Juliet on the cool sepulchre, we fuck Cleopatra in the dust at Actium . . . blowsy, fat, tawny –'

Beaudricourt 'Blowsy'?

Kate For '*échevelée*'?

Beaudricourt 'Blowsy' . . . 'blowsy'. *Je sais pas* . . .

Kate 'Dishevelled' is closer, but you don't get certain connotations, the fleshiness, say –

Beaudricourt It's nonsense.

Kate OK, we can take out 'blowsy' then. 'Dishevelled' for 'blowsy'.

Beaudricourt No, it's all nonsense. (*He snatches the document.*)

Kate You're worried about your English. Michel, that's my role.

He's ripping the text up.

Don't, don't –

Beaudricourt Why have you brought me here? To humiliate me?

She wrestles it free.

Kate Sit down, you should sit down. It's very late. I think you should sleep.

Beaudricourt I have done my sleeping. I have slept for ten years. (*He drinks whisky.*)

Kate I thought you were on some sort of medication?

Beaudricourt This noise. Do you hear it?

Kate Is this what they call an episode?

Beaudricourt Marie, Marie?

Kate Don't wake her. Where are they? The tablets.

Beaudricourt Marie.

Kate No. And don't keep drinking –

Marie stirs and laughs.

Marie *Je suis épuisée.*

Kate I'll, I'll find them. In here?

Beaudricourt In the *valise*, yes, no, *pas là, vitement, vite,* Kate. (*He's shaking.*)

Kate Yes, fine, here.

Beaudricourt Let me –

Kate What's the dose?

Beaudricourt I will –

Kate examines the capsules.

Kate Lithium? Jesus Christ. I mean I thought, maybe, Prozac.

Beaudricourt Kate.

Kate Lithium – God.

Beaudricourt Give them here.

Pause; she looks at him.

Kate This is what she's doing to you.

Beaudricourt I am very sick.

Kate Making you fuzzy, mercurial, feeding you lethal chemicals –

Beaudricourt It is very simple.

Kate – hiding you away, eating away at your brain – it's criminal.

Beaudricourt I am ill, Kate.

Kate You are not *ill*.

Beaudricourt Well, you must tell this to my doctors.

Kate Someone should. This is how the great get neutralised.

Beaudricourt Do you hear it, these bells and the water? (*He is shivering.*)

Kate There are solutions and you can take them – you are the strongest man I have ever met. The very strongest.

Beaudricourt Is this sound inside me or outside me or where is this sound?

Kate Don't talk – just breathe. With me. Slow. Deep.

They breathe together.

Get your feet on the ground. OK, yes, listen to this sea. See it.

Beaudricourt *Oui.*

Silence except breathing.

The British sea.

Kate I think it's the Irish Sea, actually.

Beaudricourt Ocean. Without shape. Open, open.

Kate Good, good. Talk about that.

Pause.

Beaudricourt When I was a boy, six, I wrote my first text, in my *cahier*, in, er, invisible ink, just a poem, you know, nothing, a *bagatelle* . . . in Breton.

Kate Concentrate on your breathing.

He nods.

Beaudricourt In Breton, which was forbidden by them, they would beat you for speaking this 'dialect', the *professeurs* were all collaborators, *petit-bourgeois* – I cannot seem to tell this story.

Kate Are you feeling clearer?

He nods; he embraces her.

Beaudricourt Yes, a prose poem; very fanciful, but I remember it, now, now, why? 'The Extraordinary Voyage of Saint Illtud.' A poem in the style of Victor Hugo, in Breton, by Michel Beaudricourt, aged six. To be memorised by heart and recited in secret. (*He laughs hoarsely.*)

Kate Recite it for me.

Beaudricourt No, it's reactionary, foolish –

Kate Don't censor yourself.

Beaudricourt 'The first Bretons were sailing men of great courage, men from Cornwall, from Wales, men who braved mighty waves in tiny boats, bearers of the word in exile, round the rocks of Finisterre, in little barques so frail . . .' (*He falls silent.*)

Kate That's good. Talk like that, talk. Your mind is so – undiminished.

She holds him. Marie wakes and laughs.

Marie *Ah, les amants.*

They separate.

Beaudricourt *En Anglais.*

Kate *Non, non, je prefère* –

Beaudricourt *J'insiste.*

Marie *C'est pas L'Angleterre, mon cher.* (*She sees the drugs.*) You should have woken me. The dosage is exact. And there must be no drinking. *Dieu*, you should have woken me.

Michel starts putting on his coat.

Kate I don't think he needs them. I think they are an irresponsible prescription.

Marie Michel, are you trembling? You have the tinnitus?

Kate Besides, he needs all the clarity he can get. For tomorrow.

Marie You are a doctor, *mademoiselle*?

Kate And I believe he has the resources, the inner resources.

Marie Michel?

Beaudricourt I will swim. In the sea. (*He starts to exit.*)

Marie It's three in the morning. You are in a town you do not know in a country you do not know. You must sleep, you need to sleep. Besides, the sea frightens you.

Fulton rubbing face, stretching, half-dressed in towel. Paces with notes and dictaphone.

Fulton 'It would seem that a grammar-school boy from an obscure Midland town – Midland market town – (*Stops watch and tape.*) – Check mercantile status of Stratford-upon-Avon – (*Restarts tape and watch.*) – who took himself to London to seek – (*Stops; restarts.*) – to eke out a living in a nascent art form – no – in a commercial enterprise rooted in the entertainment of lordly patrons and the riling of puritanical censors – it would seem that the hastily assembled bulk of his largely extemporised plays, laden with news bulletins, jester-jigs and date-stamped jokes – good, good – (*Stops, checks watch; rewinds, plays back.*)

Dale stirring from sleep, Fergus at lap-top.

Dale What? What you doing?

Fergus Desperate, shitty scholarship.

Pause.

Dale Well, I'm – sleep.

Fergus Yeah, you stay beddy-byes, I'll just – keep – fucking up – here.

Dale Dreaming. Nice dream.

Fergus I fixed you breakfast.

Dale Dream about a beach. Off Route One.

Fergus There's a beach here.

Dale No, not a beach, 's – what – a deposit – this, this was a beach – sunlight – someone holding me – pines, white sand.

Fergus Here, breakfast.

Dale drinks coffee.

Dale Cold.

Fergus OK: 'The intellectual axis of English cultural and political –'

Dale 'S not England.

Fergus To all intents and purposes.

Dale It'll piss people off.

Fergus You know a Welsh intellectual axis?

Dale You want the faculty chill-out again? Greasespots, Jesus.

Fergus 'The intellectual axis of British cultural and literary –'

Dale Toast is cold, too.

Fergus Dale, I've six hours to get the opener –

Dale Butter's intact on – the bread.

Fergus I need back-up here.

Dale It's four a.m., I don't do four a.m., I don't do back-up before sunrise.

Sign: BIRMINGHAM NEW STREET. *Waiting room. Six a.m. Sandy reading Gwynn's paper.*

Gwynn Don't bother with that now if you don't feel in the mood.

Sandy Well. I'm just . . . browsing. Dozily.

Gwynn Sure.

Sandy I thought it left at six.

Gwynn Yes. Platform Eight, depart: six a.m.

Sandy Well. (*She looks up and moves around, stretching.*)

Gwynn So, initial response?

Sandy I like it.

Gwynn Yes?

Sandy Yes. (*Hands it back to Gwynn.*)

Gwynn Great.

Sandy Come along, little train, don't keep us waiting.

Gwynn You felt it was, you know, well founded?

Sandy Very well founded – I mean your bibliography . . .

Gwynn I tried to cover the field –

Sandy You certainly do that. (*Shouts.*) We've bought a bloody apex ticket and we made reservations.

Gwynn So too many references?

Sandy No, no, I think the references, and there are . . . a few – are necessitated by . . .

Gwynn Did you mind me referring to your . . . manuscript – I felt I wanted to say that.

Sandy No. No. Very flattering, always ready to be flattered. Definitely Platform Eight?

Gwynn Platform Eight, six a.m. Definitely.

An inaudible station announcement.

Kate and Marie alone.

Kate We should go after him.

Marie shrugs.

Kate He's . . . impulsive.

Marie Michel is a child. In this state. That disturbs you?

Kate Look, I want you to know that . . . that I didn't expect, I didn't imagine you would come.

Marie Were you disappointed that I did?

Kate I was under the impression – this was to be a chance for him –

Marie Michel?

Kate I think by now it must be clear to you, Marie, that things are changing . . . I'm sorry, I must go and sleep and – (*Kate goes to leave.*)

Marie Don't go. Stay. Let us talk.

Kate I'm sure you can't stand the sight of me.

Marie But that would be terribly vulgar. Stay. Perhaps you can assist me.

Kate With what?

Marie offers her back; Kate helps her undress.

Marie Besides there have been many others.

Kate Naturally.

Marie You at least are pretty. He finds it hard to discriminate.

Kate His past's well documented.

They look at each other.

Marie Yes, you seem to have done your research on us.

Kate I don't actually make a habit of doing this sort of thing. I didn't set out to . . . hurt anybody.

Marie laughs.

Marie My dear I am beyond hurt. Michel and I are less fragile than you suggest. But of course I will die soon so . . .

Kate You seem in formidable health.

Marie No, it will happen soon. I am an old woman. You are young. You can learn from me how to tend him.

Kate I'm not intending to be his bloody wife.

Pause.

Marie He insisted I came. I always come.

Kate Michel?

Marie nods.

Marie He is a creature of habit. He has his routines, as we all do, of course. But without them he is formless. Attention must be paid to his *toilette*, his status rewarded with signs, wherever we arrive, to create the necessary patterns. And of course his medication, and of course to protect his . . . peace. A life's work. Work you make difficult.

Kate I'm simply offering him space, choices you've closed down.

Marie You disturb him profoundly. And you bring him here amongst strangers. To this godforsaken province.

Kate It's a chance to relaunch himself, to break some new ground.

Marie His career is over. He must learn only silence, *sagesse*.

Fulton taping, lying on floor.

Fulton 'These worldly, timely texts, innocent of their later cultural centrality, these throwaway squibs, tailored seamlessly to the hungers of a heterogeneous audience who drifted into the Globe as idly no doubt as any Saturday afternoon multiplex viewer, rooting for Shakespeare over Jonson as casually as they now root for Screen Six over Ten-Pin Bowling' – (*Stops tape.*) – Check multiplex attractions – (*He launches into sit-ups.*)

Station sign: SHREWSBURY. *Sandy seated with lap-top, Gwynn with bottle of Coke and a muffin. Seven a.m.*

Sandy This is getting stupid.

Gwynn They reckon big delays. Hours maybe.

Sandy We're talking about a train journey across seventy-odd miles of a so-called developed country. I only said I'd do it as a favour.

Gwynn Par for the course.

Sandy Did they fare any better on the catering?

Gwynn One double-choc-chip muffin. I thought we could go halves.

Sandy I couldn't, really.

Gwynn Oh, it's the usual flooding, up Machynlleth way. The track goes right down by the estuary and –

Sandy There's no such place as McCuntleth. I refuse to believe in such a place.

Gwynn Oh yeah. Little market town, hippies, wind farms and the like.

Pause. Gwynn eats the muffin.

Sandy We'll be lucky if we get to the plenary at this rate.

Gwynn We'll be lucky if we get there at all. There were mutterings about a service bus from Oswestry.

Sandy Fuck. Sorry. I don't say that word but, you know, fuck. God knows how Fergus lives in these shitty, sorry, but these shitty little places, I honestly don't know.

Gwynn I grew up in Aberystwyth, actually.

Sandy Yes, you did, of course. How patronising of me.

Gwynn They didn't have Diet Coke, just straight Coke.

Sandy swigs from the Coke.

Sandy Poor Fergus. This'll scupper his bid for glory.

Gwynn He needs some too. Looked him up on the web; could only track down a couple of articles.

Sandy Yeah, well, nevertheless. Always my favourite lecturer.

Gwynn I'm sure you gave him a run for his money.

Sandy Hardly. I knew nothing. I was the girl who did her homework in advance, the one with the handwriting so neat you could eat it; and Fergus was, well, this troublemaker, queer before it got fashionable, badly exploited by the College, holed up in this drafty little cubby-hole whiffing of sherry – pink shirt, gorgeous after-shave (still smell it), those sort of thin wiry Euro-specs, books in heaps, everywhere, in French, Italian, little coffee-maker, obscure volumes of poetry and theory – Beaudricourt, the whole set of them. Yes, that was my education, breathing the air in that room.

Gwynn I shouldn't think he was a patch on you though – as a supervisor.

Sandy Sure he was chaotic; missed appointments, didn't read stuff. Fun, though.

Gwynn So were you. I was so chuffed when you agreed to be mine.

Sandy Well, I've always been an advocate of mature students. This Coke's flat.

Marie looking out of the window, Kate with books.

Marie I must find him. He has these attacks.

Kate You underestimate him – worse, you undersell him; he's at a turning point – in the anglophone world, certainly, he has never been more – I mean, read all this – (*She selects a book.*) Reprints. New editions.

Marie The last time we found him, the police and I, his lips were blue.

Kate OK: *Oppositions to Freedom* – (*Reads.*) – 'Navigator of the wilder reaches of contemporary sexuality', that's a, a Booker prize nominee there –

Marie Again, some lover. The same pattern.

Kate Or *Prisms* – 'cartographer of the new maps of the self' –

Marie Ah, *des bêtises*!

Kate Or in art catalogues, quoted or misquoted in Sunday supplements, I think I even heard him name-dropped on MTV at one point – *(She laughs.)* – I mean he's in the culture!

Marie You celebrate his castration.

Kate And I tell you what, *madame*, I happen to think *After the Gods* will be – is – a triumph, a triumphant return to form, yes.

Marie You lecture me on this – *bagatelle*, this suicide of which, because of which I suffer, since ten years. This word 'suicide' in words.

Kate Posterity is going to judge you harshly for suppressing the early drafts.

Marie *Mademoiselle*, I care not for 'posterity', I care for a man. I have loved this man forty years, loved him – *totalement. Sacrifice totale – tu comprends, ma petite – le jour, la nuit.* I nurse him sick, hide him in triumph, catastrophe, silence my womb for his peace – fight with left, with right, with agents, publishers, newspapers – all the, all the maggots that – eat him; I have read each word he writes even, yes, yes, even *billets-doux* to the – women, creatures who stick on him, who he grows sick of *encore et encore* –

Kate I am not some bloody little whore, is that what you're suggesting, some groupie, I – I –

Marie You go to these wild reaches with Michel, his wild reaches, no? You learn lessons I teach. Look at you, you could take *les jeunes, vous êtes jolie, pourquoi chasse un homme qui ne peu pas être dur? (She laughs.) C'est absurde, vraiment.*

Kate *Pour vous, madame, peut-être.* With me he cried afterwards – for what he had forgotten, for what he rediscovered.

Marie slaps her face; Beaudricourt re-enters, wet.

Beaudricourt The sea is very cold.

Fulton now pacing and speaking.

Fulton '. . . this naive body of texts buried under the rubble of four centuries of interpretation, subject to secondary and tertiary accounts, subject to commentaries on commentaries on commentaries – (too many commentaries?) – commentaries on commentaries – and now granted the attention of Michel Beaudricourt, whose name clutters the indexes, footnotes and prolegomena of all those who' – ride the wave? Suck the teat? (*Switches off tape; shaves.*)

Fergus works on, Dale draws near, massages neck.

Dale That good?

Fergus Great. Down there a bit.

Dale You're like cable.

Fergus Here: 'The intellectual axis of European . . . blahblahblah . . . is shifting westward. Theory, once quarantined at Calais –' (Is that good – no, no, bogawful.)

Dale Dip your chin. And up. And on your chest. And up.

Fergus '–. is now the new paradigm in progressive literary studies. The plate tectonics of continental discourse have ruptured the pack-ice of English humanist –'

Dale Metaphor mixage. Plus this English thing is back. Lie flat.

Fergus does. Dale moves down his back.

Try 'Anglo-Saxon' – go for non-Celtic oldness.

Fergus Good – the race thing too. Oh Christ, yes – right there.

Dale Transatlantic.

Fergus Sounds regressive, yes – oh, that's – good – 'Anglo-Saxon humanist *positivist* pack-ice –'

Dale stops massaging.

Dale Isn't Fulton re-thinking positivism?

Fergus Fulton is history; Beaudricourt will take him apart – I've programmed them consecutively. Fucking two-round knock-out, boys. Hit the canvas, Fulton, you go down.

Dale Your anger's kind of pathological, Fergie.

Fergus I am *not* angry.

Dale Your face is puce.

Fergus Puce?

Dale Just at the guy's name.

Fergus Don't get on the jealousy jag.

Dale Jealousy?

Fergus Dale, I have colleagues, I have old students, I have little parasitical bastards who still need my imprimatur, I have one or two guys I mistakenly mixed business and pleasure with.

Dale You're in protestation overdrive. Puce.

Fergus I am not puce, OK. I am pale and fucking interesting. As ever.

They suddenly laugh. Dale sings Bowie: 'Breaking Glass'.

Dale (*sings*) 'You're such a wonderful person.'

Fergus (*joins in*) 'But you've got problems.'

Dale 'So let me touch you.'

Fergus OK, enough already.

Goes back to his work.

Dale Fun over.

Sandy and Gwynn under new sign – MACHYNLLETH.

Gwynn As a Welsh woman I feel I should apologise for this.

Sandy I don't hold individuals responsible.

Pause.

Gwynn You're quiet.

Sandy Sorry.

Gwynn Don't be.

Sandy This is what happens when I sit still too long. In come the moods.

Pause.

Gwynn Talk to me about them. I should warn you, I'm a trained counsellor.

Sandy I don't accept the ideology of counselling.

Gwynn Some people are too clever for it. Try me, though.

Sandy Oh dear, you know: 'What separates me from death?'

Gwynn Death's a long way off, I would have thought.

Sandy Yes, yes it is. I see things stretching before me. More of the same. More unread books and half-baked seminars.

Gwynn Unread books? Come on. You're in paperback.

Sandy OK, sure. But for whom? For whom?

Gwynn Your work is terribly important. Look at me.

Sandy Yes, it's self-indulgent, yes. I don't normally talk about myself, I –

Gwynn I'm not saying that. I just mean you're in your prime!

Sandy Not for long. Yes, look at you – and all those who come after.

Gwynn I'm ten, no, fifteen years behind you.

Sandy Yes, but your output – two sons, marriage and a book on the way. How do women do this?

Gwynn That's just life not – output – that's just blundering along.

Sandy The difficult bit, I think.

Gwynn Anybody can have kids. God, it's all some of us can do, yeah. My niece's seventeen and she's just got knocked up.

Sandy That's very young.

Gwynn I was only twenty-two, first off. It's what you do to compensate for going nowhere. Husbands being the other thing, right.

Sandy This is not about children and husbands. I'm not in the market for that, clearly.

Gwynn No, no. But I bet Beaudricourt hasn't got kids.

Sandy Oh no, not him – propagates through text, not genes. (*She laughs.*)

Sandy And how is he? Your husband.

Gwynn Glyn? He's – well, he's – well, we . . . we've . . . separated.

Sandy Oh. I'm sorry.

Gwynn No, no, it's . . . good.

Sandy But you've been married donkeys years –

Gwynn He – we haven't spoken the same language for ages. Literally, sometimes.

Sandy But your sons.

Gwynn They went with him. They chose to.

Sandy Gwynn.

Pause.

Sandy Is there another woman?

Gwynn Doubt it. Don't much care.

Sandy Is there another man?

Pause.

Gwynn I don't think that's my territory any more.

Sandy Your territory?

Gwynn This is ridiculous. Saying . . . this. To you. (*Gywnn is tearful.*)

Sandy Oh. Well. Are you – 'out'?

Pause.

Gwynn I am now.

Inaudible station announcement.

Dale dressed, Fergus half-dressed, still working.

Dale We should cater.

Fergus I doubt he'll be kicking around.

Dale As there's not a decent restaurant in town. Pot-luck supper. What's the story for lunch?

Fergus Salads.

Dale Do something indigenous.

Fergus You forget. The Welsh have no cuisine.

Dale There's fish. I'll get some fish. Keep it simple and tasty.

Fergus I'm attempting to think here.

Dale Red mullet. Does Beaudricourt have dietary requirements?

Fergus I wouldn't know.

Dale He's French, connoisseur of the body, of appetite. Red mullet, butter sauce, butter and parsley sauce – how's that?

Fergus Dale, I am labouring to bring forth . . . stuff –

Dale Fergus, these people have travelled distances. Hospitality is essential.

Fergus They're paid the going rate.

Dale It's getting the stuff in. Can't hump it from Safeway. Can we get a taxi? Why don't we even have a car, why do we live in a town with serious gradients, no mall and absolutely nothing in the way of glamour?

Fergus stands.

Fergus I don't need the problems, Dale – I have the problems – try and put this shithole on the map and – shit – from all quarters – jobsworthshit, Cymrushit – partnershit –

Dale Partnershit? I have carried you these past –

Fergus I haven't time for a domestic, Dale, honest to God –

Dale Oh 'domestic', right, great, fuck you then –

Fergus Leave it *alone*.

Dale – good, good evasion strategy, the work as smokescreen, usual strategy –

Fergus I am not hearing this –

Dale – to evade the facts, yes –

Fergus OK, facts, Dale, OK – *the facts* – two fates – for me – for us; fast-track or slow-death – the fast-track is fast receding, yeah, the book is fucked –

Dale It is not fucked, it's . . . imminent, it's –

Fergus It's a running joke, OK, and the Principal of this – pile, the University of Aberystwyth for shite's sake, has called me, to my face, 'Research Inactive' – *to my face* – facts, Dale – I came in with promises, the clock is tick-tocking, and definite fact, we cannot *live* on you swanning off up the Rhinogs to write your sonnet sequence.

Dale That's – I resent that. Jesus.

Silence.

Fergus I'm sorry.

Dale Yeah.

Fergus It's just – this conference is the last ditch, Custer-style – if you want out, you get me that job at UCL, at UCLA, get me those jobs, Dale – or – or – give me back-up.

Dale sighs.

I'm running out of options.

Dale You've got options. You're a Young Turk.

Fergus I'm thirty-eight.

Dale A teenager.

Fergus I'm not . . . respected.

Dale You have connections. Fulton, Sandy – both top-flight, fast-track. You get mentioned in their acknowledgements.

Fergus That's the past.

Dale Well – what am I – what can I say? – Jesus I – I wash my hands of this lugubrious – this – I am not equipped to detox this – lugubrious – Jesus!

Beaudricourt stands; the women watch.

Beaudricourt I failed.

Marie You're feverish.

Beaudricourt Stood at the water's edge. Removed my belt. (*Laughs.*) 'Sans-culotte.' The sea like a black beast and my fear.

Kate It would have been lethally cold in there.

Marie is towelling him down.

Beaudricourt Yes, it was cold, Kate. Cold enough to wake your bones, your heart.

Kate You're in wet clothes though, now. You should change.

She starts to peel his top off; he shudders.

Marie He's shivering.

Beaudricourt Let the darkness come down. (*He places Kate's hand on his face.*)

Marie Take your medication, please.

Kate Perhaps, Michel, perhaps she's right.

Beaudricourt You wake me with a kiss and push the pillow on my face.

Kate Maybe this is premature.

Beaudricourt No, I have never lived, I have read books and written books and advocated dangers.

Kate Yes, we want your ideas, we're not after gestures.

Beaudricourt Even in '68 when history was with us, I stayed inside words. The crowds frightened me, disgusted me, yes, I find people rather disgusting, my old students with their ridiculous hair, their beards, the unwashed girls, kids who had queued for my seminars now booing, chanting.

Marie You had a longer view, *chéri*.

Kate You're still fighting. These people are civil servants now!

Beaudricourt I have created nothing of value – founded no ethics, no planets, no regimes. *J'ai griffoné – griffonner?*

Marie *Je sais pas.*

Beaudricourt *'Griffoner'?*

Kate Oh. Doodled.

Beaudricourt Doodled – doodled in the margins.

Marie You are speaking wildly now and foolishly.

Beaudricourt No, I am lucid, full of light.

Marie *Michel, prends tes médicaments et demain matin nous allons rentrer chez nous et ta traductrice va dire: 'Michel est complètement désolé mais'* –

Kate Speak, no you speak you keep going.

Marie Darling, *prends ta médication, je t'en prie. Je veux dormir. C'est tard.*

Beaudricourt Tell her, Kate. Tell her I am still well. Tell her. I am well. Tell her I am young, yes, still young. Inform her of the hope I still have. What you have seen in me.

Pause.

Kate We have to be up early. We really ought, all of us – I mean of course Michel, of course, but –

Marie I will pack.

Beaudricourt *Oui.*

Kate People have come to hear you.

Marie *Ici, chéri.*

He takes a pill.

Kate What are you doing?

Marie You should go. We will refund any expenses, of course. I know you will be discreet, but I think it is appropriate to mention Michel's illness.

Kate You will . . . disappoint . . . many admirers –

Marie We have found in the past that Michel's work has no real audience in the Anglophone world.

Beaudricourt They confuse me with Sartre.

Kate He's forgotten. Sartre's forgotten. Completely and utterly.

Beaudricourt You knew Sartre? No, you could not – ugly, fish-eyed. Paris was silent when we buried him. Waiters in doorways hard with respect. I walked behind his coffin cursing him.

Marie An irreplaceable loss. Here.

He takes another pill.

Kate You are fêted everywhere, cited everywhere –

Beaudricourt I have had many translators. I have been traduced in all languages.

Kate Not before with love.

Beaudricourt Non! (*Spits out drug, sits on floor.*)

Marie Leave. Please. I – I don't want you to see this.

Kate He's –

Marie *Je t'en supplie.*

Kate Not before with love.

Marie *Va-t-en.*

Kate I'm going. Michel. I'm –

He's silent.

Marie Sssh.

Pause. Kate exits.

Fulton on phone.

Fulton Emma?/ Who's this?/ Is that Lizzie? / Lizzie is that –? / Yes, it's your father / Daddy, yes Daddy / could you fetch Emma? / Mummy? / yes / no don't / oh / could you pick it up again? / Lizzie, look I really have to speak to / I haven't time / Daddy hasn't time / DON'T put it down / what, what do you want to – / I don't know that / DON'T / I'm not shouting, I'm not angry I just want / no crying now, Lizzie, please / OK, OK. (*Sings.*) 'The big ship sails on the Alley-alley-o / The Alley-alley-o / The Alley-alley-o / The big ship sails on the Alley'/ Lizzie, that's all you get now, I'm getting angry here / yes I am because I wish / don'tdon'tdon't / good girl / hello? (*Checks watch.*) / oh Emma, don't let the girls answer the phone, if possible, people do call, in a hurry, like myself, anyway, anyway, I don't want to get into the child-care conundrum, I'm just calling I'm just, basically I can't get back tonight / no / trains all over the place and besides, business to transact, dinner / look I don't relish this, Emma, I am not seeking the petal-path of adulation, I can assure you I shall not be popular after my little valedictory / my paper, yes, my paper / I'll do my share of wet-wipes on return, love? / Love? / Emma? / Yes? / I wish you wouldn't question it. (*Phone down; he looks at it angrily.*) I don't deserve you. (*Suddenly rubs his face, and jogging on the spot emits what sounds like a war-cry.*)

Fergus dressed in suit, Dale in coat.

Fergus How do I speak to him?

Dale You'll be cool.

Fergus Is he 'sir'? *Monsieur*? *Professeur*? Michel? What do we talk about?

Dale You'll be totally cool.

Fergus His work? *My* work? He's probably difficult, tetchy – and why did he come – I'm not even Welsh – the guy bested Foucault on telly, talked policy with Mitterand, partied with Bardot! And here's me, fucking eejit from TCD, blagged my way into EngLit as cod culture-provo, fecking nowhere-man, odd late-night radio slot, odd published newsprint shite, résumés of the impact of Post-Mod on – what was it?

Dale Museum lay-out.

Fergus Even quoting your man there – and Fulton – never phones, never answers e-mails, and Sandy, who's like the essence of Political Rectitude right down to her masturbatory preferences – they're going to take me apart.

Beaudricourt on floor; Marie stands.

Marie *Ah. Bien. Michel, aides-moi, je veux dormir, et mourir.*

He snorts.

Michel, je suis fatiguée je veux mourir.

She tries to hold him, he pushes her away.

Je t'aime.

Pause.

Beaudricourt *J'ai pas besoin de ton amour.*

Beaudricourt shaking, Marie cradles him.

Je suis un monstre, un autre, oh – je suis un autre –

Marie *Je t'aime. Que moi, que moi – moi seule, moi seule, moi seule.*

He seizes her, shakes her with great ferocity.

Beaudricourt *Je te déteste, immonde, monstre, monstre, monstre, tu me tues, tu me tues, tu – tu, tu me tues.*

Beaudricourt forces her in a hug onto the bed burying her face into a pillow holding her, her cries stifled.

Fergus paces, Dale tries to hold him.

Fergus I am out of time and I am just – I'm clearing out, tell them I had – a bereavement, I'm on the B-and-I to Dun Laoghaire –

Dale Fergus – look at me, honey, look at Dale, honey, gorgeous Fergie – hey – now – Beaudricourt is coming to your conference. Yes. Fulton has committed public allegiance to you – many times. Yes. Sandilya is your very good friend. Yes. I, an accomplished poet of some repute, have chosen you for my lover – everything else is garbage, everyone else is nobody. Fergus, this is glory-time, apotheosis time, you are about to become godhead. (*He kisses him fully.*)

Fergus Ah Dale, you're truly beautiful sometimes. Truly.

They exit.

Beaudricourt on bed with Marie, who's still. Silence.

Beaudricourt *Marie? Marie. Tu dors. Pardon. Pardon. Tu dors? Marie?* (*He shakes her.*) Marie. (*Lets her fall back.*) Oh. (*Pause.*) Oh, oh – *c'est pas possible.* Marie.

Blackout.

Act Two

ONE

Aberystwyth University: two settings, an exam office, where lunch is served on a round table; and three podia at the front of the stage. As the scene changes, we hear Fergus, Gwynn and Sandy's speeches cut into each other, all played directly out to the audience.

Fergus Do fill up from the front . . . don't be shy now. (*Pause.*) Couple of bits of housekeeping – the back hall Ladies is out of commission, thanks to some student misogynistic prank, couple of disgruntled rugger-boys got the wrong grades 've apparently left some handy may-fly eggs in there to hatch, which they duly – did – anyways, we're all in there together, folks, and gents, you're requested to not use the urinals – actually, maybe we should have a show of hands about that?

Gwynn The following paper attempts to address the claims of theory in general and Beaudricourt in particular as 'prisms' through which the 'texts' of Shakespeare (and here I take 'text' in the sense of the Beaudricourtian 'text', that is, an unstable cross-weave of ideologies without any assumption of closure or final meaning) – sorry – the 'texts' of Shakespeare – Shakespeare being, as Beaudricourt notes in his forthcoming – I hope forthcoming – a – please excuse my French, linguistic education at Aberystwyth Secondary had a fairly parochial bias – '*un nom divine*' – this is Shakespeare – '*un site, un oracle*' – a site, an oracle.

Sandy I want to talk about courage, cultural courage, the courage to face Others , outside yourself, inside yourself; the courage to unthink the boundaries that mark us, inside and outside our heads; with nation states that bleed all over the world, immigration officers posted in distant airports, Europe as permeable as a membrane, the boundaries are within us as much as in border posts. And we need guides, we need Calibans who know the lingo, who have the courage to cross over and Beaudricourt is, was, such a Caliban, guiding us through this new landscape, forging, in his early work at least, deeper and deeper into the Queer forest, as his courage held; now he balks at this isle 'full of noises', fears, perhaps, his own castration deep in the uterine darkness of Cleopatra's Egypt, where Europe stands inverted, where his home, his matrix, *la France* herself, lies transfigured, Marseilles fused with Algiers, French South and African North one realm, the realm of Sycorax, that silenced immigrant from the Maghreb. But I'm not here to disparage those early heterosexual, Eurocentric journeys into the interior; no, I say let's go further, deeper, let's take forward a pennant with which Queer and post-colonial subjects may claim their new domain.

Fergus Professeur Beaudricourt has not yet been positively sighted – probably impounded at Dover under quarantine regulations – but I do have in my hand a piece of paper, a fax in fact, from the man in question wherein he professes his keenness to travel '*ferry Britannique*', 'retracing the epochal voyage of Saint Illtud' – and if you know who that fella is, see me after – and announcing his desire to berth at the very site of Shakespeare's *Cymbeline* – although Gareth Roberts, hi Gareth, in Modern Languages, tells me, that was Milford Haven, which these days is mostly an oil terminal.

Gwynn Clearly I am not the first to ask these questions and tribute should be paid here to other early – theoretical engagements – say, the invaluable tradition of psychoanalysis – yes, Cohen's 'Hamlet's Inversions', or Stone's 'In the Lacanian Mirror: Questioning Juliet's Hymen' – yes, or the very rich vein hit by my colleague, Dr Sandilya Pandit, who has, I think, courageously, dragged the 'Bard' into the territory of Gay and Lesbian polemic in her 'Come, Sweet Death – Re-figuring Shakespeare's Erotica' – not in print yet but, having myself been privileged to read an early draft, a truly vital, er, inspiring contribution to the debate. (*She looks up.*) Do feel free to ask any questions, methodological or substantive, raised by this paper.

Sandy For Queer critical encounters, theory is a speculum used to reveal the secret spaces of Shakespeare's great uterus, to release the buried casque of dangers and delights therein, to shatter the crust of meanings tradition has imposed to suppress the joyous body of the text – when Iago talks of Cassio's sleepy leg-over, we imagine Othello's unbidden erection; for us the asp that Charmian, Iris and Cleopatra swoon over is the dildo that ruptures their Eden; in our Forest of Arden we permit 'sweet Phoebe' to have her Rosalind whilst Celia looks on; for to read the text after Beaudricourt is always to re-read it, to re-fashion it, bursting Shakespeare's limits asunder to accommodate our newly articulated desires.

TWO

The exam office – a round table. Plates of pre-served salad laid out. Dale laying out cutlery, champagne glasses; Fergus standing.

Dale Should I lay him a place?

Fergus Use your initiative.

Dale Travel in hope, Fergus. Good turn-out too. Quite a buzz.

Fergus They are here for one reason alone and that reason hasn't fucking showed, so can we drop the optimism.

Dale OK. I'll lay for five.

Fulton enters.

Fulton Ah. I'm not early, am I? Not according to my registration pack.

Fergus Hello, Stephen.

Fulton Fergus. I don't hug, incidentally.

Fergus Ah, a good firm hand instead.

Fulton A recognised signal of good intent.

Dale And a secure masculinity . . .

Fulton (*looks at Dale*) We haven't been introduced.

Fergus My partner, Dale Stillman – poet.

Fulton A poet? In the enemy's camp.

Dale Oh, I don't happen to see it that way.

Fulton And are you a poet in print or a hobbyist?

Dale Absolutely in print. Vanity presses worldwide. I have a readership that reaches double figures.

Fulton That's practically mass circulation for a poet. (*He checks his watch. Pause.*)

Fulton How long do we wait?

Fergus You tuck in. By all means.

Fulton I mean before you reschedule.

Dale He'll be here.

Fulton OK. Nice to have such an obliging . . . partner, Fergus.

Dale laughs.

Fergus Still got your bite, Stephen. I thought family life would smooth you out a bit.

Fulton It makes compartmentalising easier. And I see you've finally settled for monogamy.

Dale That's his story.

Fergus You've no cause to doubt it, Dale.

Fulton It's growing old. Experimentation's for folk in their twenties.

Dale You make love sound dull.

Fulton Not dull, just workaday.

Dale And I guess for you that means kids?

Fulton nods.

Lucky you. Are you a good dad?

Fulton I try my best. I didn't come here to talk fatherhood.

Dale I find it interesting. Y'know, viewed from afar. Fergus doesn't go for it.

Fergus strips cling-film off the salads.

Fergus Oh look at this bollocks – I requested a salad, OK, so we have here 'salad', that is iceberg lettuce, at its most fecking liqueous –

Sandy and Gywnn enter.

Sandy So this is what passes for high table? I wondered where you were lurking. Fergus, a kiss please.

They embrace.

Fergus Hi, love. Top marks for the speech.

Sandy Patronising swine. And sorry I missed yours. Blame Ivor the bloody engine.

Fergus Yeah, you cut it a bit fucking fine, didn't you? I was vamping for you.

Gwynn We had to literally run from the station.

Dale It was a beautiful entrance.

Sandy And this is the lucky guy we've all been hearing about?

Fergus Yeah, Dale, my prop, my other half.

Dale He keeps my shoulder permanently soggy. Nice to finally get to meet you.

Sandy Yes, likewise.

They shake hands.

Fulton Hello, Sandy.

Sandy Stephen.

He leans in to kiss her awkwardly.

Smart as ever. You remember that woollen suit he used to wear all the time, Fergus. Even in high summer.

Fergus And brogues, for God's sake. Aged twenty-one.

Fulton You'll be amused to know I still have them.

Fergus Was he a dandy or a fogey?

Sandy Oh, a definite fogey. You must have met Gwynn, Fergus.

Fergus Yes, hi. I tell you what, forgive me for this, I thought you were a bloke.

Gwynn Oh. Well, I'm not. A bloke.

Fergus No, I mean having just come across you in print.

Gwynn Yeah, well, as you see – very much not a bloke. But don't you worry about it.

Pause.

Sandy Where's the man himself?

Fergus He's declined as yet to materialise, the bastard.

Sandy He's on in half an hour.

Fergus Precisely.

Pause.

Fulton I found your paper elegant and entirely meretricious, Sandilya.

Sandy Well. Good. Got something right then.

Gwynn It was a pity the women were programmed simultaneously.

Fergus Yeah, well, my mistake, as you know.

Dale I actually enjoyed your paper. What I could get of it.

Fulton It probably appealed more to a poetic sensibility than a scholarly one.

Sandy Do your worst, Stephen. How did yours go, Gwynn?

Gwynn I got the overspill audience. Yeah, and it was pretty dry, I find it hard to strike the right note.

Sandy You're just rigorous.

Gwynn Oh, and nobody asked any questions.

Sandy That's probably a good sign.

Gwynn shrugs and sits down.

Gwynn Do we get anything to drink?

She opens a bottle of wine and pours it out for everyone.

Fulton Are we permitted to eat this little spread?

Fergus Yes, do eat, eat – help yourself – er – yeah –

Gwynn drinks rather rapidly.

Gwynn That's sharp stuff, that.

Fergus Well, take it steady.

Sandy No, we can be naughty now, can't we, Gwynn? We're done.

Gwynn That's right.

Fulton If he fails to show I could go it alone, I have plenty of material –

Fergus Well, maybe. Christ. Why not?

Sandy New work is it, Stephen?

Fulton Absolutely.

Sandy Exciting. Do you break any new ground?

Fulton Oh I think so, yes.

Kate enters.

Kate Sorry? Is this the speakers' lunch? This is the panel?

Fergus I'm sorry, this is a closed lunch for invited parties only –

Kate You must be Doctor O' Connor. You've not had word of Michel?

Fergus Michel? Are you a delegate?

Kate I'm his translator, Kate Leverhulme, hello.

Gwynn Hello, Kate. Would you like a drink?

Kate No thank you. (*to Fergus*) I think we spoke on the phone.

Fergus He's here?

Kate Yes. Well, no. I mean if he's not here. Which he isn't, is he?

Fergus I don't see him.

Kate I suspect – given his state last night –

Fergus He got here last night?

Kate I'll be frank with you.

Fergus Time somebody was.

She takes him to one side.

Kate He's not well. In fact he's very very unwell. Which he apologises for, yes, he would like you to know that he is very sorry but . . . but he is unwell and has had, will have to return – prematurely – to France.

Fergus He has signed contracts. Binding contracts. And the fee went out upfront.

Kate Well, I suspect this isn't at the forefront of his mind, but I'm sure he will reimburse you for any losses –

Fergus People here have travelled distances, have shelled out considerable sums; has he checked out of the hotel – where's he staying?

Kate I couldn't raise him. He sleeps very heavily. Probably the medication.

Fergus Well I'll gladly rock over there and give him a little wake-up call.

Dale Fergus, if he's not well, then –

Fergus If he's acting the fickle fecking primadonna on us now – we paid over the odds and on expenses, we paid way over the odds –

Fulton It wouldn't be the first time; there was that debacle at Oxford.

Kate I'm very very sorry – for – sorry – you know, I'm – sorry. On his behalf.

Fergus OK. He's due on in twenty minutes. Time to break the unwelcome news. I think, maybe if Stephen, you give your paper and we – open it up to the floor – and I could – do a reprise –

Gwynn We could have a sort of panel discussion. General sort of chat.

Fulton I'm not sure chat is the order of the day.

Fergus Yeah. Whatever. Look, eat this stuff will you, eat this crap, eat it up, eat it.

They turn to the food. Beaudricourt enters, dishevelled, wild.

Kate You're here.

Beaudricourt *Bien sûr*.

Pause. Dale starts clapping; they all join in.

Beaudricourt Please. You embarrass me.

Kate Are you OK? Sit down.

Beaudricourt *Comment? Oui, oui*. Please, we should eat, eat, I believe we, I am due to – talk.

Kate You shouldn't go ahead with this –

Beaudricourt I have my speech. I have things to say.

Kate No, we didn't finish the speech. Where's Marie?

Gwynn Who's Marie?

Fulton Monsieur Beaudricourt always travels with his wife.

Pause.

Sandy *Professeur*, I'm excited to meet you. Sandilya Pandit. You're in all my bibliographies and most of my footnotes.

Beaudricourt I do not charge for citations! No. I consider my work . . . the property . . . of all.

Gwynn You should, you'd make a packet –

Sandy Sorry, this is –

Gwynn Gwynn – Thomas. Doctor.

Fulton I hope we're past pulling rank.

Gwynn I want to say I have found a lot of your stuff so – you know – heuristic. And not just on the page. In life too, in life. Have some wine, it's pretty good.

Beaudricourt Yes, yes. (*He turns to Fergus.*) Ah, my English ambassador. We met when he was a postgraduate, you were a boy in your spirit, you have aged, my friend –

Fergus So they tell me.

Beaudricourt Always, I remember, after my seminars, he would ask these impenetrable questions in bad, bad French. My ambassador.

Fergus God, that's a responsibility. I apologise right now for any misrepresentation.

Pause

Dale *Bonjour, Professeur.*

Fergus Yeah, sorry, this is Dale my – partner.

Beaudricourt Your partner? Ah, your lover, perhaps?

Dale Right. (*Laughs*.)

Fulton As no one is offering, allow me to re-introduce myself, Professor Beaudricourt, I –

Fergus You've presumably met Stephen Fulton before?

Beaudricourt Fulton. Fulton. Yes. You wrote – superbly – once – yes – but now?

Fulton I am, as you know, a great admirer of your work – but these days I feel I must take issue with its influence and consequences.

Beaudricourt Is a work's value not measured by its impact on the world it enters?

Fulton I don't believe of course that one can hold great individuals responsible for the manner in which they are appropriated by – lesser – individuals.

Sandy Is he talking about us, for God's sake?

Fulton And how is Madame Beaudricourt – you know, I made her acquaintance, eight or so years ago, on a rather misguided pilgrimage to Brittany – you were indisposed – she made me welcome, we drank coffee, ate *brioches* – she even offered me a bed – I declined – is she well?

Pause.

Beaudricourt You seem very interested in my domestic arrangements.

Fulton Yes, yes, as she – well I expected . . . that she might attend –

Beaudricourt It is the spirit of the times to make puerile, reductive links between public and private life. Must we blame feminism, *mesdemoiselles*?

Kate A certain hysterical form, perhaps. Speaking as a post-feminist.

Gwynn That's bollocks really. I couldn't read a book the same way if I knew the author was, I don't know, a wife-beater or something.

Kate Is 'bollocks' a technical term?

Fergus Start applying that criterion and we'd all be out of a job.

Gwynn I take back 'bollocks'. I'm old-fashioned; ask Sandy about some of the literal, moralistic stuff I used to come out with. I apologise for saying 'bollocks'.

Sandy Besides, Michel, you have encouraged this approach in some ways, certainly you dismantled the boundaries between biography, text, ethical discourse – in *Oppositions* –

Beaudricourt Thirty years have passed since that text – you were a baby at its conception –

Sandy But your conclusions there have been very fruitful – your celebration of a literature of Desire unencumbered by disciplinary 'Deities' of belief systems, of –

Beaudricourt A pretty *précis*.

Sandy 'Pretty'?

Fergus Let's have some of that bubbly? Dale?

Dale Excellent. Safeway's finest fizz. (*He fetches some bottles from a carrier bag.*)

Fergus Oh, it fizzes. Here: courtesy of the University of Aberystwyth. They don't own farms, ecclesiastical property or gold plate, but they get some subs from Cardiff and so we get plonk that fizzes.

Gwynn You don't knock this place, OK; this place is a miracle, this place was built and paid for by miners, preachers and farmers, my grandfathers. So don't you knock it. I just had to say that.

Pause.

Fergus Perhaps you should do the honours, then.

Gwynn OK. Do I shake it up? No, it's hardly the Grand Prix – oops.

Gwynn opens a bottle, it fizzes wildly, spraying over Fergus.

Oh God, I'm sorry.

Fergus Leave it.

Gwynn wipes him down.

It's fine. The shirt's only silk. Shit.

Dale takes the bottle and pours glasses out.

Beaudricourt Charming. (*He looks at them as if for the first time. His eyes fill with tears.*) Many thanks. My friends. Many thanks. To you and the Welsh . . . (*He turns to Gwynn and embraces her.*)

Gwynn (*giggles*) Well . . . I can't speak for the whole of Wales.

Beaudricourt As you of course know, as a Breton I am in fact Welsh – no paradox. Who were the first Bretons, Dr O'Connor?

Fergus I'm dodgy on the Celts.

Gwynn The Welsh, the Cornish. In flight from Saxon shits. Saint Corentin, Saint Illtud, Saint Malo –

Sandy Gwynn! How do you know all this stuff?

Gwynn Comes with the terrain, I guess.

Dale We should propose a toast. Fergus.

Fergus OK, OK. A toast to the work of a true intellectual – whose revolution burns slowly in the mind!

Fulton Sounds horribly painful.

Laughter. They eat and drink.

Fergus It's unfortunate, Michel, you missed Sandilya's extremely exciting paper which made compelling claims for Queer theory as building on your foundations – well I shouldn't attempt to, er –

Sandy And Gwynn's paper too – she makes fascinating use of *Prisms*.

Beaudricourt Forgive me – I forget my early incarnations; one is always in a landscape defined by the coming text. Frankly, sometimes, I feel sick at the idea of my *oeuvre*, it weighs on me like earth, like fat – and, yes, Monsieur Fulton, I fear at times I have erred on the side of ecstasy rather than illumination. Yes.

Dale They can be the same thing. You said as much.

Beaudricourt I said this too?

Sandy The debate in *Prisms* over bodily knowledge –

Gwynn The body as a privileged vessel for –

Dale Thinking through desire.

Gwynn In *Prisms* –

Fulton The premise most fully explored in *Oppositions* –

Beaudricourt You batter me with my words. Invent your own. My words are not unassailable. (*He gropes for medication in his briefcase.*) Don't look at me. I am not a courtesan. (*He counts out tablets.*) The mind – one becomes aware increasingly that the mind is circuits that die out, chemicals that . . . dry up.

Kate You're running low.

He waves her away, takes the pills.

Beaudricourt Please, talk to me of Shakespeare. He is your poet – how must I read him? Tell me how I must read him.

Long silence.

Fulton We're out of the habit of talking of Shakespeare – extempore.

Fergus We don't actually have very long –

Beaudricourt I ask with absolute humility. Shakespeare.

Pause.

Gwynn God, where do you start?

Pause.

Sandy OK. When I was sixteen I was cast as the Indian boy in *A Midsummer Night's Dream,* the school's annual play. I wanted to play Hermia – but the teacher, the director, who I sort of – loved – and the cast – thought that would be 'unrealistic' – for me to to play that part – as I was the only 'Asian', indeed the only non-white in the place – so I would stand out too much, as Hermia, whereas I wouldn't in the *non-speaking* part of the Indian boy – and it would further this 'realistic' approach if I played this Indian because I was 'Asian' – like him. My parents were pleased at my being cast in the play whatever role, because they felt this was an 'opportunity' for me to – fuse – better with the 'majority' – before that I had resisted being defined as an 'Asian' and had said I was 'British', indeed had got sort of ashamed of my parents being 'non-British' – I mean, I never experienced any overt racism at this school, which was in many ways a model girls' grammar – but when I auditioned for the *Dream*, as we all called it, everyone agreed my voice (which I usually made as toneless and Brummie as the rest of them) *came to life* – as I read the verse – 'came to life', as the teacher, the one I fancied, said, in an 'incendiary' way – that fuelled my hopes for the coveted roles of Hermia, Helena (or, as it was a single-sex school) Oberon or Puck; so when the cast list was pinned to the notice board and I saw myself down for the non-speaking part of the 'Indian' boy I – cried – in the corridor – I wept – and the teacher took me to one side and explained that she had been constrained by the demands of 'realism'.

Pause. During the next, Beaudricourt consults his text.

Gwynn That's so bloody sad. So bloody sad and so typical of this racket.

Sandy It wasn't meant to make you feel sorry for me.

Gwynn You sometimes think education, now, the whole business of it, is just about pinning you down. You go there, you do this, this is for you, this is not for you. And so you get students coming to classes and it's 'Literature's crap' or 'What's the point of Shakespeare?' and it's tragic when you think of the fight we had just to get any sort of education, y'know, I mean go down town and you will see the reading rooms, you will see the subscription libraries, the chapels, places built from the pennies of the poor, mostly closed down now or turned into thrift shops, you know there were struggles here, everywhere to learn, to *know*, in fact it's funny for me coming here 'cos I can still recall the first time I came into this building, I was twenty, doing some godawful job, utterly bored in the way most people have to be and there were these classes here so I just came along 'cos OK, I'd read a bit and had no one to talk to about it and you think you'll meet someone so I went along – and in all my time growing up in this town I'd never set foot in here, never even thought you just could – so I come in and there's some chap doing a talk on *Antony and Cleopatra*, dry as dust, can't recall any of it except one thing, a line of text, which he reads pretty indifferently – 'I am again for Cydnus,' yeah – says it very slowly, 'I am again for Cydnus.' And you know what, there and then, that very second, I knew I had to go there, to that place, to Cydnus. And I didn't care much how I got there.

Pause.

Look, excuse me.

She blunders out; Sandy stands.

Sandy She's having a tough time of it, I think.

She goes too. Pause.

Beaudricourt We aren't fit for Shakespeare truly, we aren't fit for tragedy.

Fergus It's time.

Beaudricourt I can't read this. (*He discards his text.*)

Kate Michel, you have, it is imperative that you . . . the Professeur has produced a seminal paper which the conference should not be deprived of –

Beaudricourt No. It is mendacious, what is that word, that English word – frippery. In the circumstances.

Fergus If you'd have sat through the nonsense I trotted out earlier, you'd not dispense so lightly with . . .

Beaudricourt Frippery.

Pause.

Fulton We could offer a dialogue in its place. A loosely chaired discussion. Fergus, you could lead it. I mean if it helps.

Beaudricourt A dialogue?

Fulton Then questions. Fergus?

Fergus Well, OK, but we must start. A dialogue, then, Michel – in lieu of your paper?

Kate This is a mistake.

Beaudricourt A conversation amongst peers. What harm can words achieve? Please – *on-y-va*.

They nod.

THREE

The podia. Fulton right, Beaudricourt left. Fergus at centre.

Fergus For this closing session, at the request of the two speakers we're going to adopt a more informal *tête-à-tête* style and consider the implications of Professeur Michel Beaudricourt's work for literary studies and the apex of the canon, Shakespeare, one of the so-called gods that Michel's new book apparently takes on – so on my right (and please don't read the usual geo-politics into that), I'd like to introduce Dr Stephen Fulton – Stephen and I used to pore over Michel's work back in the eighties and I promise you whatever he says today he was lit up by it then – his PhD was – is – still –

Fulton 'The only comprehensive account in English of Beaudricourt's writings on literature.'

Fergus He's never been shy, has Stephen –

Beaudricourt A major work. The major work in English.

Fergus There, high praise indeed – OK – but Stephen is renowned for his rigour, some say restlessness, and in recent years he has perhaps retreated into more empirical territory –

Fulton I rediscovered certain Anglo-Saxon verities.

Fergus 'Anglo-Saxon verities' – good name for a folk band – anyway, on my left, a figure who needs no introduction except to recite again the names of texts that we've all fed off these last thirty years – *Prisms, Oppositions to Freedom, Racine:Rousseau:Roussel* – and the forthcoming examination of issues in contemporary authority – *After the Gods*. Welcome, Michel, to Aberystwyth. Perhaps, Michel, you'd like to kick off, and say a little on why Shakespeare, given your previous concern with linguistics, the avant-garde novel, political rhetoric, pornography – admittedly Racine, but then merely as a paradigm for . . . so why Shakespeare?

Beaudricourt Good afternoon. Where to start? (*Pause.*) First, yes, I wish to apologise as a Breton that I do not have any Welsh – I would like to speak to you in Welsh but . . . so I speak as a Frenchman, as a Breton in fact, as one therefore who approaches Shakespeare with dread. His silence in French is a terrible absence, his presence in English is an awesome heaviness. So I wished here, and in my work, as always, always I have done, perhaps too many times, perhaps, to, to commit a form of sacrilege, of profanation, I wished to talk from within Shakespeare – within Shakespeare, whose face one looks into as if – Narcissus, gazing into his pool, rapt – seeing in Shakespeare's face one's own, reflected, held in the light sent across the years from his 'mirror held up to nature' –

Fulton Professor Beaudricourt, if I might come in here and perhaps inject a note which I often feel is absent, some might say repressed, from your work, and indeed the work which you have – generated –

Fergus Perhaps Stephen we should alternate through the chair – but –

Fulton Of course –

Fergus Well, please, you were –

Beaudricourt Please –

Fulton Well, I was referring to the absence of a certain material dimension, shall we say, a lack of concern or indeed interest in the facticity of these texts which, after all, did not spring from the void – let us remind ourselves that we are here to discuss the works of a grammar school Midland boy from the mid-sixteenth century – an operator in a commercial field, the theatre, a man of his times writing for the men of his times – I'm stressing here, you see, the fresh, provisional nature of the work, the life, its soil of fact, reality, something of a taboo word amongst my colleagues – and a soil that seems not to feed your – meditations – I don't know if you feel this to be a lack –

Fergus Let's be honest, Stephen, you are advancing here a polemic against theoretical engagement as such – surely you're not suggesting that, at this late point in the consideration of the Shakespearian –

Fulton Excuse me, I'm sorry, I was hoping, perhaps that the question might be passed over without mediation – Professeur, in your literary – excursions – you have disregarded fact, context, history, method. Do you feel these absences?

Beaudricourt Absolutely. Yes, yes it is a lack, an absence. But then the facts are – past. This only (*Indicates a text.*) remains. Words alone, which are still in a process of becoming, changing. And our own context, our own history which we bring unconsciously, like our shadows, to the text, reading always in our time, from our time, and we reshape 'Shakespeare' (who I speak of not as a person, not as William Shakespeare, but as a figure, a site, an idea – yes a god) to the language and needs of this time – because text only remains.

Fulton Yes, of course, the context is lost, but for scholarly endeavour the great, the perennial task –

Beaudricourt But I am interested in this after-life of text. This . . . corpse which still . . . speaks. Of death.

Fulton Death? A somewhat reductive reading. There's more to Shakespeare than death, more pressing concerns: kingship, ownership, nationhood.

Fergus Death as a metaphor for the constant loss of meaning, perhaps.

Fulton Ah, the flight to metaphor!

Fergus Excuse me?

Beaudricourt No. Death is the spur of Shakespeare . . . Shakespeare, this charnel house. Murders – parricide, fratricide, regicide – murders – Shakespeare articulates our constant desire to kill, to die – he makes us again and again, watch, want, desire the moment of despatch. Ah, my brother Hamlet, kill Claudius at prayer, stop his mendacious search for grace, plunge your poniard into Polonius there behind the arras, good, 'dead for a ducat', good; yes, kill them all, end this play, even kill yourself, achieve your 'quietus', yes, a 'consummation devoutly to be wished' –

Fulton Again I must point out, I must raise the question of your method, this virtual re-writing of the text, mounting in criticism, perhaps lazily, the constant rehearsal of what concerns us *now*, seeing the plays as some kind of pretext for –

Fergus I think it might make more sense and would be more valuable to allow the Professeur to complete his –

Fulton – and as a consequence, inevitably, rediscovering, as Dr Pandit puts it, our 'newly articulated desires' in all places rather than what is literally *present* in the text – dispensing with the tiresome issue of intentions, value, say, meaning in the sense of bounded – I mean you handle this magnificently, you have this great talent for dissolving boundaries, fixities, which I, on the other hand, increasingly feel to be necessary boundaries, necessary *thresholds* –

Fergus You invoke notions of form, convention, boundaries – in criticism, or in life – I sense more than an aesthetic, I sense a creeping morality –

Fulton Absolutely. Nothing creeping about it. A morality of reading, a morality of action. Michel, you have been somewhat pushed to the margins here. Do you wish to –?

Beaudricourt Yes, yes – (*He stands up.*) Yes, Shakespeare speaks to us – yes, indeed I am inside Shakespeare, deeper than any . . . actor. 'Playing' Othello. I am Othello, here, this hotel room now the palace at Cyprus. Looking into the – blanched – face of my Desdemona – limp in my hands – her fine old hair spilling out, her mouth open, astonished, there, her small blue tongue.

Pause.

Fergus Michel, we have, rather, strayed –

Fulton Typically in fact -

Beaudricourt I have killed my wife. With these hands. (*Pause.*) That is to say, I found her dead – let us be clear – let us be clear there was no – no calculation – let us be clear – *je ne peux pas plaider la folie – je vais – je vais – oui –*

He stumbles off. Fergus stands. Silence.

Fulton Perhaps I – Fergus – I could revert to –

Fergus I hardly – think it's possible in the –

Fulton I would very much like, and I'm sure the conference who travelled distances, paid money to –

Fergus I think conference feels –

Fulton You have no right to censor me –

Fergus It is not a question of censoring –

Fulton stands, starts to read his lecture notes.

Fulton 'I wish to share with you a nauseating vision; but of course you are familiar with it, you live with it, a vision of tiny academic territories receding into smaller and more futile specialisms –'

Fergus I think the moment has passed.

Fulton What I have to say here is highly pertinent – springs indeed precisely from this admission of lunacy, a lunacy generated by this vertigo of 'commentaries on commentaries on commentaries –'

Fergus Stephen, you're making a tit of yourself –

Fulton You fail completely to understand your *function* as chair, you have had your say at some considerable – here – 'I wish you to share this vision, our lives squandered on tiny, futile specialisms, academic territories receding into –'

Fergus Shut up for God's sake shut right up.

Pause.

Fulton OK. This is why this speech serves as my valediction. I am going into the real world of real work, a world where I can earn a living doing something I don't despise, where value is created not traduced. What I wanted to say can be simply expressed – thus – (*He tosses his papers into the air and walks out.*)

Fergus stares forward; he laughs.

Fergus Well, in the immortal words of the Bard – that's all, folks.

Blackout.

Act Three

An empty lecture hall, a podium downstage, with entrances upstage and downstage left. The room is high in the campus building, lit by windows constantly buffeted by wind. Sandy sits on the floor with her lap-top; Fergus stands, speaking into a mobile phone. It's about five p.m., the light fading through the scene.

Fergus That's actually incorrect – factually – that's, I'm sorry, that's pure speculation – pure spec – he is of course infamous for his ambiguity, his blending of genres – seamlessly fusing autobiography, critique and a sustained, creative use of allusion – well you must print what you heard, clearly – I understand that I – I only ask that you – I'm merely adding my penn'orth so – no, no charge for citations no – you're welcome – welcome – OK, OK, cheers then, yep, cheers. Pleasure. Pleasure. (*He calls off.*) Fucking arse-festival of arse-fucking-shite.

Pause. Sandy looks up from lap-top.

Sandy Shouldn't we be cautious about this?

Fergus About what?

Sandy Shouldn't we perhaps consider our status –

Fergus With regard to what?

Sandy I think we should. Look.

Fergus wanders over to Sandy's lap-top.

Fergus Who are we to thank for this?

Sandy University of Essex site. Unsigned.

Fergus Essex. Jesus.

Sandy Shall I read it?

Fergus Let's hear the worst.

Sandy 'Confessions are cool in theory-speak, but no one thought Dr Anti-Humanist Beaudricourt would go *cri-de-coeur* on us; *blague* or *nouvelle vague*? Or confirmation that Frog misogyny rules OK'.

Pause.

Fergus They're glib fuckers in Essex.

Sandy They've drawn their conclusions. This is where I think – I mean, what is our status? Witnesses? Bystanders? Accessories?

Fergus To what?

Sandy To what!

Fergus We heard a man we admire give an **incoherent** speech concerning mortality, moving, shambolic, perhaps lacking past rigour, with a coda – a wake-up call –

Sandy A coda! Fergus – please –

Fergus Yes, a coda, a provocation.

Sandy An explicit confession of murder –

Fergus Whoah, hang on, just – wait – no one, nobody is talking murder, whatever actually happened – no mention, I think of –

Sandy Killing then, killing, he said, 'I have killed . . .', you know.

Fergus Words, yes, to that effect, but, **given the** *context* – guy's clearly fucked up, mental meanderings, guy's a pale shadow of his former –

Sandy Stated. In plain English. No subordinate clauses, no qualifiers. No adjectives even.

Fergus Did I teach you nothing, Sandy? Was there ever ever an innocent statement of fact, ever in the entire history of the world? There was not.

Sandy I think, Fergus, you're being just a little ... evasive –

Fergus Words, Sandy. Language.

The phone rings.

Sandy Leave it.

Fergus What?

Sandy I just think everything you say takes you ever deeper into this ... swamp.

Fergus I'm simply clarifying –

Sandy Fergus, you're doing his work for him, you idiot.

They let it ring off.

Fergus Where's Dale got to? Everyone pisses off when things get sticky. I thought we were going to debate this. I thought maybe we could form a committee, take some kind of collective action. But everyone has trains to catch. You can't just go back to things, Jesus wept. Even whatsherface, Miss Wales, where's she got to?

Sandy We said we'd meet here. She knows people here. She had the bloody tickets so I'm stuck now.

Pause

Fergus You could kip with us. You could stay a bit.

Sandy Well. Thanks.

Pause.

Fergus It's nice to see you, in fact, y'know.

Sandy Yes. (*Laughs.*) You look so much older, Fergus.

Fergus Oh. Ta, babe.

Sandy We all do. But I do worry about you, at times.

Fergus Really? You don't need to worry about me, I'm . . . all right.

Pause

Sandy I always boast about you, you know, and you still have this incredible cachet amongst – my peers . . .

Fergus Then it sort of dries up, does it? With the youngsters? Who's that old bollocks, O'Connor? Big in the nineties, right? The early nineties, to be precise.

Sandy What, what happened to you though? Your book was always being puffed in catalogues, always about to be printed. I felt confident, I still feel confident it would have been, it will be – definitive.

Fergus I'm glad you still feel that.

Sandy I mean you're hardly lazy or complacent.

Fergus I started that bastard thing as a young man. Now it's the work of a stranger. Every day, early every day, I go to my desk, start to read, re-read, go back to the preface, read it back, the confidence amazes me, yes, yes, go forward, stop, re-read, now it's wanky, over-pitched, claiming stuff you could never pull off, the words crawl, don't add up. I have a coffee, a smoke, go for a walk. Back to Chapter One; disaster – in 1989 the jewel in the crown; I recall writing it, the day, the place, kind of thrill passing through me – my territory, nobody else has been here or thought this, y'know, and it's big shit, it matters; now heaps of stuff says the same thing, says it better, worse, just says it, my students, your students, and it's dull, obvious as fucking daylight. OK, then there's

Chapter Two – which I gave tentatively as a paper, '95, somewhere, sounds OK, but Fulton's there, leaves me on the floor after questions, shreds me, my premises, my material, have I read so and so's excellent such and such, hasn't the time come to go beyond . . . blah blah; still taste the dryness in my mouth, like salt. Or read it to Dale, even fucking Dale's bored, he doesn't say, he won't say, no, but I know. I wasn't made to bore people, that's not my talent, Sandy. I tell you I feel like I have a stiff stored in my room, I don't go in there, feel like I'm going down into my own fucking grave in there. (*He is crying.*)

Sandy Oh Fergus.

Fergus Forget it.

Pause.

Sandy I had no idea.

Fergus Good. I'm glad of that.

Sandy Anyway, at least you're fixed up and not shrivelling away like some of us.

Fergus What?

Sandy Dale.

Fergus Oh yeah. Dale. He certainly picks up the slack.

Sandy You seem able to lean on him.

Fergus Yeah? Well we don't all have your autonomy and calm, sweetheart.

Sandy Oh, I am far from calm, Fergus.

Pause.

How do you think he did it?

Fergus Did what?

Sandy You know.

Fergus Don't dwell on . . . this.

Sandy I keep seeing his hands. His rather large hands. There must be some considerable strength in them.

Fulton enters from downstage entrance.

Fulton So. You're still here. Hello.

Fergus Ah. Right.

Pause.

Fulton Just the two of you, then.

Sandy Yes. Sorry.

Fulton Sign of the times. Imagine all this in the sixties. They'd be passing resolutions, forming committees; now they all slope off muttering.

Fergus Thought that was your plan.

Sandy You made a very final-looking exit.

Fulton Oh, that came across, did it? Good – not yet, not quite.

Fergus More to say then, is there?

Fulton There's always more and after all I didn't quite get to say what I came to say. What with your guillotine motion – and of course, the ultimate in exit-lines, our former hero's revelations. I take it he's former for you too now.

Fergus Oh God, I've heard quite enough of this shite for one day.

Fulton What's keeping you here then so . . . spell-struck – ethical paralysis, perhaps?

Fergus You're the paralytic one, pal – been at the mini-bar?

Fulton Dutch courage is all. Fergus – before embarking on a bit of primary research – yes – fact-checking, empiricism.

Sandy What are you jabbering about?

Fergus Don't expect sense from him –

Fulton I went back to the scene of the crime. Not this one, the other, the one with the victim.

Sandy What? The hotel?

Fulton The hotel.

Sandy Did you find . . . her?

Fergus Don't indulge him.

Fulton I sensed we'd been in the same lodgings – unsurprisingly s'pose, there's only one hotel to speak of and it's not much to speak of. There was some brouhaha last night I remember – late, late – I couldn't get off –

Sandy Did you find her?

Fergus This is futile.

Fulton I asked at reception – was she in – Madame B.? – would it bepossible to speak to her? Yes, she was in. But strict instructions had been left that she should not be *dérangé* – by her husband. My face was a mask of discretion, Fergus, you would have admired me for it. No comment. I merely took the room number and stood by the door. In the corridor.

Fergus Is this meant to titillate us?

Sandy Sshh! Was he there?

Fulton No. Just me. It was quiet. Unearthly quietude. I knocked. (*Giggles.*) 'Knock, knock.'

Fergus (*seizes him*) Look just – say whatever, what you – just –

Fulton Oh. Struck those tender nerves then. Good.

Fergus lets him go.

Sandy And what else?

Fulton That's it. (*Lies down on the floor.*) Didn't know what to do with my deduction.

Pause.

Sandy God – it's all true.

Fulton I'm a bit dizzy.

Fergus Is that the sum of it?

Fulton Fergus, you look . . . so old.

Fergus Can we cease this fucking old business?

Fulton Doesn't he, Sandy? Remember how glamorous he once seemed?

Fergus Spare me the nostalgia.

Fulton I place you and Michel together in my mind; filed away there – do you, Sandy?

Sandy There are rather more immediate concerns. Good grief.

Fulton I feel sad all of a sudden.

Fergus You're all over the shop. Sit up. Come on – up – you'll puke or something.

Fergus heaves him up; Fulton lolls on him.

Fergus Oh look at you.

Sandy picks up the phone.

Sandy – what – don't be ridiculous –

Sandy dials.

Sandy Emergency services, presumably.

Fergus Sandy, we cannot adjudicate here. We are only bystanders, right? If that –

Sandy Hello – police, please – they're routing me through – I need a script –

Fergus What exactly are you going to report?

Sandy I'm sorry, could you repeat that? / Yes / Sandilya Pandit / Dr / Is that really necessary?

Fergus The police, for fuck's sake, when it comes down to it. The police!

Sandy S-A-N-D-I-L-Y-A. / Look, this is complicated / no, no immediate danger, no –

Fulton Ah – the forces of authority –

Sandy (*off phone*) Shut up / no I'm not involved in any immediate . . . look could / I'm not sure I like your tone / could you pass me to someone / and you are? / the desk sergeant, well, I'd like to speak –

Fergus You see – you have nothing positive to –

Fulton Weasel words.

Sandy OK, OK, let's have your number (Fergus, pen – pen!) / write this / 776290 / I can assure you I will follow this up. (*phone off*) Absolutely outrageous. Pedantic, sinister questions . . . they routed me through to God knows where –

Beaudricourt enters downstage, stands silent.

Fergus Michel.

Pause.

Beaudricourt *Évidemment.*

Fergus Come – come closer.

Michel approaches.

Sandy Fergus, wait – think about it. Professeur, I think it's only fair to you before we get too cosy to . . . that you should be aware.

Beaudricourt Yes?

Sandy I – we – are in the process of contacting the authorities.

Beaudricourt I see. *Bien sûr.* I wondered if Kate . . . but I see she is not . . . I will . . . leave.

Sandy I imagined – I hoped you might have given yourself up.

Beaudricourt I wish this was easy like it sounds.

Fulton I would imagine it was pretty straightforward. You go to the police.

Beaudricourt I have been to your police, yes.

Sandy They didn't take you in?

Beaudricourt They were – busy – with immediate concerns. A man and a woman fighting, drunk. One officer. When I spoke, he mocked my English. Invited me to contact Interpol.

Fergus Ah, the great British bobby.

Beaudricourt So. I come instead to you. My colleagues. My peers.

Silence.

Sandy You understand that everything is changed between us.

Beaudricourt *Naturellement*. May I – sit?

Fergus Yeah you . . . do that.

Beaudricourt Thank you. I am very tired. Very tired. A long day and night – *je sais pas. Je sais pas. Je sais pas.* (*He starts to undress.*)

Sandy What are you doing?

Beaudricourt *Sais pas.*

Fergus Michel. You don't have to do this.

Beaudricourt *Sais pas.*

Fulton Very good, very good. Expiation now.

Sandy This is – quite – superfluous.

Beaudricourt, in underwear, holds his belt out as an offering and stands.

Beaudricourt Punish me. *Je vous en pris.*

Fergus Michel, please, put your clothes back on. Let's take this a step at a time – let's talk this through and get you – please –

Beaudricourt Punish me. (*Pause.*) *Maintenant.*

Beaudricourt holds his hand palm up and lashes it with the belt several times.

Beaudricourt *Et là, et là – là – voilà – là – oui –* so, so – *là, là – ah – là –*

Fergus For God's sake.

Beaudricourt *Je suis sordide – là, et là – bien, bien –* (*He attacks his back, putting about himself with the belt.*)

Sandy Stop it, stop it, stop it, just stop it.

Fergus You're hurting yourself.

Fergus and Sandy try to disarm him. He crumples. Fulton watches.

Beaudricourt Your duty, your task.

Sandy There has to be due, due process – there has to be law and –

Fergus Absolutely right – the law and its processes –

Fulton (*quietly*) The law. Yes.

Beaudricourt Oh law, law, I am far from law, I am wrong, I must suffer sufferings, suffer here horror here here – icicicicicici – (*He pinches himself, bites himself.*)

Fergus No no no – NO –

Sandy Please, Michel, please –

Fulton For Christ's sake –

Beaudricourt Ah – 'Christ' – (*laughter*) – Christ! *Bien, bien* –

He tries to tear at his own flesh, they pin him down.

Fulton Hysterical.

Fergus You're in no state to –

Beaudricourt *Je suis monstre, vil, merde,* shit, *je suis* shit. Shit.

They hold him down. He stills.

Sandy We don't even know the precise circumstances of whatever happened between you and – your wife –

Beaudricourt You want a confession? Then, what – you – absolve me – *et puis?*

Fulton We're in no position to forgive, to absolve, nobody could.

Sandy Perhaps if you gave an account –

Beaudricourt *Non*. Words, stories, commentaries – *finis*.

Fergus It might at least help – to be clear, fair to yourself and –

Beaudricourt No. Explaining – *non. Néant*.

Beaudricourt stands. They hover.

Sandy So, so you – killed – your wife. Yes?

Beaudricourt nods.

Sandy You killed her. With your – just your – hands.

Beaudricourt Yes. (*Pause.*) Continue.

Sandy That's it. That's all.

Fergus We don't have the facts, well, we do but we don't have – what the facts amount to.

Fulton Fact. A body is decomposing in a hotel room.

Fergus God.

Sandy A woman's body. How old was she?

Beaudricourt Seventy.

Fulton Your wife of forty-odd years.

Sandy Forty years. Your whole life then, lost.

Beaudricourt No readings, *madame*. Facts alone.

Pause.

Sandy Why did you kill her?

Fergus That's not a helpful question. I don't think.

Beaudricourt I cannot say. There must be reasons.

Fergus Just pure, just an accident –

Sandy I'm not sure there's such a thing –

Fergus He was pissed, sick, he was pigsick and low.

Fulton You were intoxicated. Not yourself.

Beaudricourt (*laughs*) My 'self'. Yes. Drunk. Drugs, of course. Sick. Alibis. No.

Fergus Oh we drink, yeah. God, you just do. Gotta shut the machine down someways.

Beaudricourt Banal. Banal.

Fergus Can't get off at night sometimes – thoughts fecking whirling –

Sandy Unhappy perhaps. At heart.

Fergus I mean, even you reckoned yourself a failure, you, Michel, despite a world's evidence to the contrary.

Fulton Well, one's work can . . . disgust. The lies, the folly.

Silence.

Beaudricourt Yes. Yes. Correct. Continue.

Sandy She, your wife, she reflected back, this disgust.

Beaudricourt No. Marie was – was? – *toujours* – more –

Fulton She confirmed it at least. Compounded it.

Fergus Just reminding you, daily, of what you'd let slip.

Beaudricourt *La vie perdue.*

Sandy Her life, too. Finally. Who was she?

Pause.

Beaudricourt She read the papers to me, I had no stomach for news. She, she read to me. Her rage – turning the pages. So. So. This, and this, and this – the crimes, Chechnya, Iraq, Congo, Palestine; crimes of structure, the brutalities. *Tous les jours, les journaux.*

Fergus A militant.

Beaudricourt My reader. My best reader. Everything I wrote, read. The things we suppressed – read – years of pages and ideas. *Tous les mots, tous les jours.*

Sandy But – who was she beyond you – and your needs? This woman?

Beaudricourt Beyond me? *Je sais pas.*

Pause.

Beaudricourt When she was a girl she carried messages – for the *maquis*. Hidden, see, like so, in a fish, a *baguette*. Through checkpoints. Holding in her mouth messages. *Visage – vide – aucune expression.* Young, not pretty, but *juste*, fire of justice. (*Pause.*) *Et bien.* The past. (*He's tearful.*) Oh and she cooked – *bien sûr*, for me, but I think for her, yes, her joy, her pleasure. Her hands, red, fast, her – *esprit. Des potages.* Singing, all the while.

Silence. He looks at them. He starts to dress.

Fergus Don't make the wrong decision.

Beaudricourt All decisions are now wrong.

Fergus It's not a crime – as such.

Beaudricourt Crime is movies. Crime is motives, logic. I am not a criminal, I am a monster.

Beaudricourt starts to go. They try to stop him.

Fergus Let us –

Sandy We could take you –

Fulton Don't go and –

Beaudricourt You must allow me to take – the steps. You commence work you are equipped for: the critique. Of all, all I have written.

He leaves by downstage entrance. A long silence.

Fergus What did we do – there?

Fulton Don't – agonise.

Fergus Sandy?

Sandy I'm not very – good – with – confrontation.

Fergus Really?

Sandy No.

Pause.

Fulton We gave him an audience.

Fergus You're a pretty glib proposition, you know.

Sandy Don't snipe. Now.

Silence. Sandy breathes slowly.
  Dale enters from upstage with numerous bags of takeaway food.

Dale Oh. I didn't cater for Stephen, I figured – I mean there's always something of an excess – (*He unpacks food as he speaks.*) – OK pasanda, lamb, nice saffrony rice, sag aloo, peshwari nan, touch limp but at its best sorta fluffy, somewhere between substance and air – (*He takes a bite.*) – sorry could not resist that, sorry, ah, chicken korma, biriani, pilau – eat it while it's hot, chillun'.

He gives out nan bread, which they eat.

Fergus (*starts to eat*) I am famished – in fact –

Sandy I wouldn't eat such dross normally . . .

Fulton Given the paucity of lunch.

Dale Go for it.

They all eat, except Sandy.

Sandy What have we done?

Dale I don't quite know.

Sandy We primed him.

Fulton Yes. Clarified his sense of –

Sandy I don't know –

Dale What's this? Who was here?

Fulton I'm sober.

Fergus That's good stuff, that's beautiful fucking stuff that –

Sandy I'm having a beer. Yes, I'm having a bloody beer.

Fergus Good. I'll join you. Stephen?

Fulton Why not?

Dale Wait – wait – *he* was here?

Fulton I think we gave him the courage to carry out the necessary existential task.

Fergus stops eating.

Fergus We should have gone after him. Maybe we still could – do that.

Sandy Well, I'm no adherent of Shar'ia. God.

Fergus We should have gone after him –

Fulton He needed to restore his dignity.

Dale Beaudricourt?

Fergus nods.

He came to you? Why did he come to you?

Fergus I don't know.

Sandy I don't think he knew. I mean what would you do?

Fulton He came for judgement.

Dale Judgement?

Sandy Which we were in no position to provide.

Fergus My God no, we were –

Sandy Appalling.

Dale Judgement? – who are you, any of you, any of us, who are we to pass judgement – on anybody – the guy comes to you, and, what – and you treat him to, to some *seminar* on justice?

Fulton He certainly wasn't seeking our comfort.

Sandy At the end of the day he has killed –

Dale Yes, yes, yes – unforgiveably yes –

Sandy Yes. Who could forgive –

Dale Totally unforgiveable, yes – but, but – look at us – look at us – here we all are living in total error, Fulton excluded, maybe, each of us, way off all laws, governments, institutions – and yet you permit yourself to – my God.

Fergus Dale, you weren't – there – you didn't –

Dale gets up and starts to go.

Dale, where are you going now? Dale?

Dale Where would you go to *die* in this town, huh? (*He exits.*)

Fergus Dale! You're presuming –

Sandy Go after him, he's – right. Yes, yes, he is – right.

Fergus I do not accept this description.

Sandy Oh, I feel – funny.

Fergus (*shouting*) It's easy for you, Dale, you are not *implicated*.

Sandy But, but then there's often, isn't there, this fatal softness in men, a fatal sympathy for the deeds of other men, gay or straight, especially when women suffer, yes.

Fulton It must be so wonderful to be so *particular*, so *distinct* from the rest of us – humans –

Sandy The trouble with you, Fulton, with all white European males, is it's just too bloody easy for you to move on to some new idea, some new cleverness –

Fulton White males? Are you – seriously, yes, yes, you are, aren't you – my God –

Sandy No – no – for some of us –

Fulton Us? Which us?

Sandy No, for the bulk of us, this, this is not an option, no, for some of us, the bulk of us, only the one idea, the one oppressive reality, your Europe –

Fulton Look at yourself – you are deep deep in *Europe* right up to your chaste neck, and over, way in, whatever you care to claim –

Sandy I am aware, far more aware of my role in all this, some of us, you see, have nothing to fall back on – enough, enough, I will never speak again, enough.

She grabs her coat, turns to exit; Fergus follows.

Fergus I'll come with you.

Sandy I don't need your –

Fergus OK I'll just –

Sandy Fergus, please, I need – space.

Fergus It's dark.

Sandy I'll find Gwynn . . . yes. Yes.

She exits. Fergus then follows. Fulton, alone, eats. He notes computer and mobile, looks at screen. He laughs and taps randomly on the keyboard.

He sighs, stands, rubs his face, exits – leaving the computer glowing in the dark.

Act Four

The scene moves to the shoreline of Aberystwyth. The action takes place in various locations, sparely evoked through light; the characters are simultaneously present but unaware of each other. Voices off. Kate: 'Michel', Fulton: 'Professeur', etc. Kate and Fulton enter from opposite sides of the stage.

Kate Michel?

Fulton No no. It's – hello – yes, it's – me.

Kate Oh. You're not Michel.

Fulton No.

She bursts into tears.

Kate I'm sorry.

Fulton Don't worry. I often have this effect.

Gwynn on a bench drinking. Sandy approaches.

Sandy Gwynn!

Gwynn Hey! Caught in the act, then. Hi.

Sandy Oh Gwynn. Good, good. (*She joins her.*) What are you doing out here?

Gwynn Good a spot as any. Came here all the time as a kid. Same bench. Lost track of time.

Sandy I was relying on you. I'm useless with logistics.

Dale on the shingle, Fergus enters.

Fergus Hey.

Dale Oh. Hi.

Fergus Saw you from the pier. What you doing this far up? Jesus, I had to run, I'm – (*He wheezes.*)

Dale Followed him – I thought. Turned out it was some guy with a dog.

Pause.

Fergus I'm – I feel – very fucking loopy, turned outwards – weird, y'know, wired up – sort me out, Dale.

Dale I'm not your personal drop-in centre, Fergus.

Gwynn Wine? Not very classy. Have some.

Sandy Thanks. (*She coughs.*) Warms you up at least.

Gwynn I can hardly taste it, to be honest with you.

Sandy You haven't been out here all night?

Gwynn No, no. Looked up some old mates, his and mine.

Sandy Nice.

Gwynn No, not really. They were offhand. I was boasting. Not impressed. And in the circumstances I didn't feel very impressive either. What you been up to?

Sandy Hard to say.

Kate Any news of him?

Fulton Well, I found this –

Kate You've found something.

Fulton This. Yes. Text. Handwritten. French.

Kate Here, here, let me see.

Fulton Yes, of course – I wondered if –

Kate (*reads*) His lecture. Ah. My annotations. Where did you get –

Fulton In a rockpool. (*Laughs.*) Almost placed. As if he were luring us . . .

Kate What do you mean?

Fulton Almost staged – don't you think?

Kate No, I don't think. We don't all possess your bloody – equipoise. Christ.

Dale Probably headed up the cliffs. Dived off. People do that.

Fergus You know the locale.

Dale I go up there. The cliffs, the lido, the funicular. I walk about. When you're at work.

Fergus Yeah?

Dale Yeah.

Fergus I didn't know.

Dale You ever wonder what I do when you're not around?

Fergus You write.

Dale I write! Sure.

Gwynn I saw him. Beaudricourt. Walked past me, very fast. I didn't say anything, he didn't see me. I don't like him much.

Sandy He came to us . . . we were – terrible.

Gwynn Deserved everything he got, I'm sure. Drink more.

Sandy He's probably dead already somewhere out here, drowned somewhere probably. God yes, drowned out here.

Gwynn Wouldn't be the first, might be the most distinguished but not the first.

Sandy suddenly cries.

Hey, hey. You're not kitted out for adventures, are you? (*Gwynn embraces her, rubbing her back.*)

Sandy Closer. Closer.

Gwynn stops and just holds her. Silence.

Gwynn You're amazing.

Sandy Useless, no use, useless.

Gwynn No, amazing. To me.

Sandy Don't mythologise me, Gwynn.

Gwynn I want you to know what you are.

Sandy I feel actually like a very useless and over-educated and very harsh sort of person.

Gwynn No. No. You should let me tell you what you are.

Kate I feel very responsible for all this, you know.

Fulton How responsible . . . are you?

Kate Oh utterly utterly utterly.

Sandy I wonder how you can be so certain as to what I am or might be.

Fulton Look look look! Another one. Either it got washed up or maybe – he tossed it from – up high?

Kate shrugs.

I'd say where there's text there's hope, right?

Kate His papers were sacred to him. He smuggled them out to me, stashed in the lining of his coat – to keep them from her.

Fulton Were you lovers?

She looks at him.

Do you mind me asking?

Kate Yes – as you ask.

Fulton He was – is – rather old.

Kate Are you planning a book about this?

Fulton And then his wife. His ex-wife. I'm not making a judgement as such.

Kate Aren't you?

Fulton Yes. I suppose I am.

Kate You can't be held to account for what you desire – I just go for . . . what I respect, I haven't time for mediocrities.

Fulton You do remind me of . . . myself.

Kate Oh, I'm easy to psychoanalyse, single child, older father, tick all the boxes, I just don't want the normal lies, I mean, as we only live once and we have no proof to the counter, do we, why put up with pygmies?

Fulton There's plenty of pygmies.

Kate Not in fact that I have any right to, not that *I* contribute anything of substance – at least I know that – but to be happy, to be – I need – I don't know, I'm weird, I do know how weird I am.

Fulton You need authority. Something greater than you. Something that's quite hard and ungiving and true.

Kate Yes. Very perceptive, thanks. (*Pause.*) I take back pygmies, I have a lot of time for them, the way they live.

Fulton I was the same, am the same.

Kate Stop trying to build bloody bridges.

Fulton Well stop trying to be so bloody exceptional. It's childish. Yes, I think I even wanted to become him, absorb him completely. To that degree.

Kate Oh. (*Laughs.*) Another sad groupie. Did you want to fuck him too?

Fulton Now you're being presumptuous.

Dale I've tried to leave you.

Fergus What?

Dale On, I think, three occasions.

Fergus You've tried to leave me.

Dale One time, you were away, one occasion, I walked up the coast, went inland. No plan. Just walked.

Fergus Dale, you haven't said this.

Dale A whole day walking this dirt road into hills. Lost. Trying to work out how we got to be so sad.

Fergus You don't say this, so –

Dale Met a boy, maybe thirteen years old, boy with dogs, shepherd boy I guess, yeah, sun broke out, it had mostly been wet, I was wet, stood steaming before him, like I was on fire, I felt, felt like I wanted to know him, speak to him – he led me back to the road, figured I was lost, spoke Welsh, some English, but he didn't *get* me, led me to the road, walking pretty much silently for, say, thirty minutes, bogs, moor, wood and I felt – I knew – things had to change.

Fergus What things?

Fulton So his wife, Marie, she knew?

Kate Oh yes. Rules of the game – he made that clear even after I'd merely taken advantage, one day, taken the opportunity, when he kissed me lightly, on departure, to kiss him more fully back, until he shook.

Fulton Must have been some kiss.

She looks at him.

Kate Are you laughing at me?

Fulton No, no. Just a sort of tic. Please go on.

Kate Go on? Was I going on? – Actually, can I, I – haven't talked about this, couldn't – to anyone.

Fulton We have to mourn them, mourn her.

Kate She asked me to dinner, very formal, candles, several courses – *soupe de poisson*, prepared from the freshest catch – *she* insisted I stayed the night. God, this was, what, a month ago, she was – you know . . .

Fulton Alive.

Kate Yes. (*Pause.*) Am I to blame for all this?

She looks at him. He shrugs.

(*shouting*) Michel, Michel, Michel – *C'est Kate, c'est ton Kate, Kate.* Michel. Please.

She sobs. Fulton hovers by her.

Fulton Maybe we should light a fire?

In a half-light Fulton and Kate gather flotsam and jetsam and create a fire. Sandy extricates herself from Gwynn.

Sandy I'm fine now. Thank you. Better. Thanks.

Gwynn You don't have to –

Sandy We ought to look for him. Well I ought to. Yes, I should.

Gwynn I've misunderstood this.

Sandy I don't know what you mean, really.

Gwynn I've misread you, totally.

Sandy Nobody knows anybody, Gwynn, finally, I don't even know who I am, for God's sake, finally.

Gwynn Right. Me too. Changed into someone I don't know – I wake up some days thinking, my God, I am paid to read books, to write about reading books, I am paid to do this not for photocopying or – we should be euphoric, we are *spoiled* –

Sandy Yes. You're quite right.

Gwynn Even my feelings –

Sandy We should shut up about our feelings. There's things we should get on with.

Dale Fergus. Jack in the job.

Fergus What?

Dale Cut loose.

Fergus What?

Dale Let's live. Less elevation, more air.

Gwynn But my desire is – is utterly bound up with – you. Your force, your friends, your reading lists – I've read every book, every article, I've loved every word connected with you –

Gwynn kisses Sandy. They recoil.

Sandy I can't.

Gwynn What are you afraid of?

Sandy I just don't – feel. I don't feel what you feel– I don't feel this.

Gwynn You're so lovely.

Sandy Stop naming me. Stop showing me what you think I am. I'm none of the things you say I am.

Gwynn stands apart.

Gwynn 'Course, I'm pissed.

Sandy Don't apologise –

Gwynn Just for a shred of – dignity. (*Pause.*) I should head off – you'll be OK on your own?

Sandy It's not you –

Gwynn Of course. Fine.

Gwynn goes off to the rear. Sandy lies down.

Fergus You realise, Dale-babe, we grow old, we grow sick, we retire, we depend on welfare, pensions, endangered specimens? Yeah?

Dale We have fallen into the man-traps – we can get *jobs*, Fergus – run Burger Kings, peep-shows, libraries – I don't want you ending up like him.

Fergus Who?

Dale Michel.

Fergus I'm not about to kill anybody here.

Dale No, in yourself. Worked out, dried out, spent. In terror of who you aren't. And living on, and me as padding. Quit the job, the pretence, it's time, this is the time.

Fergus I'm in this very deeply, I haven't finished what I started.

Dale Fuck finishing, there's too much seeing things through in this world –

Fergus I have defined myself through . . . salvaged a – without this I am no one.

Dale You're not here, man, you're not in this moment, you're never in this moment. (*He seizes him.*) Do you feel this? (*He shakes him.*) Huh? (*He picks up a stone.*) Is that stone or what? Are those stars, are those actual stars you see and do you see them?

Fergus I don't understand this.

Dale Are you with me here at this point or inside there? Is your heart beating like fuck and are you cold and are you half-way dead and do we only live once or what?

Fergus You *are* crazy, you –

Dale No, no, I am not I feel suddenly so *right* –

Fergus Stop shouting, Jesus –

Dale Fergus, you were gorgeous and I fell for you and we made love daily not just Bank Holidays and Reading Weeks, we lived *all* the time, not just deadlines permitting, permanent deferred deadlines, and in fact there happens to be one big ultimate fucking deadline coming up, yeah, no deferral permitted, no rewrite, period.

Kate twists Beaudricourt's text into firelighters. Fulton builds the fire.

Fulton First encounter with Beaudricourt: Fergus despatched me, second tutorial, with reading list – I piled up the texts, mostly French, piled them up on a desk in the reading room, like contraband – as if I had the key to the Kabbala, and all the rest squeaking past, they were in one world and I, another – a similiar sensation, yes, to waking in his – bed – him padding about, his cat looking at me, licking cocoa from a saucer, tape playing, I think it was Mahler, yes – the very same feeling as I read, descended deeper into the texts, like sinking into the warmth of his bed, his way of being – seeing into the heart of things, as if through glass, seeing the mechanism clearly. (*Pause.*) Do you have any matches?

Kate No. No, I don't smoke.

Fulton Me neither. So rubbing sticks then.

Fergus Yeah, yeah – I feel shagged out with – with the fiction.

Dale kisses him.

Felt that all right.

Kate Why did we bother with this?

Fulton We probably read it in a book. No matches!

They laugh.

Kate How come the wedding ring?

Fulton Married for five years. Two little girls, who I wish I was back with.

Kate I think I must have misunderstood your story.

Pause.

Fulton I am not defined by the indiscretions of my – past.

Kate No, no, you're free to become whoever you want to be.

Fulton No, that's a myth. Isn't it? I think so. Fundamentally false.

Kate I can't speak for others. But tonight at least I feel, I don't feel very free, no.

Fulton Yes, Emma's wonderful; the peace of a house in which children sleep.

Kate Yeah, come on, though – they wake up. You're just not there when –

Fulton The thing is, half the time – I don't have the foggiest – after Fergus there were only one or two little . . . experiments with . . . men. (*Pause.*) I often think that *so-called* repression may actually be healthier than – every step towards some sort of balance, every move, you hear their irony, *their* contempt for certain simple, constant things, those things that fuel, that fuelled happiness – (*He suddenly bites his hand.*)

Kate Hey – look – whoa – stop, stop that stupid – for God's sake –

She tries to pull his hand away from his mouth – he stops and walks away – pause.

You're bleeding, you idiot, you made yourself – bleed . . .

She follows him off.

Fulton I'm fine. I'm – very – fine.

Kate Of course. Of course.

Fergus and Dale in an embrace.

Fergus Oh God. Hugs and learning.

Gwynn with Beaudricourt drenched, humping him to stacked fire, she unbuttons him.

Gwynn You're heavy.

Tries mouth-to-mouth. Thumps his chest. Kiss again. Listens to his chest.

Professeur, réveillez-vous. Says she, CSE Grade 1.

He coughs, she sits him up and slaps his back.

Good, good. Another resuscitation –

She spits out salt water.

I'm snogging you.

She laughs. He coughs. She slaps his back.

Oh, good. Come on, come round.

She tries to sit him up; he stirs.

Beaudricourt Marie?

Gwynn Marie? No.

Beaudricourt Ah, Marie. (*He embraces her.*) *Ma chère.* Marie.

Gwynn No, she's not . . . I'm not her.

Beaudricourt looks at her.

Beaudricourt Marie?

Gwynn *Nous sommes – sur la plage. De Aberystwyth. En Wales.* Sum total of my French.

Beaudricourt Wales.

Gwynn 'Fraid so.

Beaudricourt *Je m'en souviens.* (*Pause.*) You – saved me. I tried to swim.

Gwynn You must have got sucked in.

Beaudricourt It was cold. Black.

Gwynn You must have got tugged back in. The undertow.

Beaudricourt You saved me.

Gwynn retrieves a lighter, attempts to get the fire going.

Gwynn Basic first aid, you know. D'you get far out?

Beaudricourt I thought my heart would freeze.

Gwynn You must swim well to get anywhere.

Beaudricourt One makes actions despite, despite the will, not to, not to swim.

Gwynn I think the body sort of takes over. Overrides your will.

Beaudricourt I wanted to die. I wish to die.

The fire starts to burn.

Gwynn Ssh. No one's helped by your dying.

Beaudricourt Even the sea refuses me.

Gwynn I don't think the sea's too fussed. I think at best we're irrelevant as far as the sea's concerned.

Silence.

Beaudricourt You know what I did.

Gwynn Not the time to go over that. Lap of the gods now.

Pause; the fire builds.

Beaudricourt Yes, we need them, these gods.

Gwynn (*chuckles*) Let's not get all metaphysical.

Beaudricourt They make us hurt. Their wound aches, and we make things to fill this wound, god-shaped words, *sais pas*, the UN, the orgasm, *la France* – other words such as these. Which do not fill the wound, make the wound hurt worse. I think. Do you . . . think this?

Gwynn I stopped thinking those sorts of thoughts. Too much like hard work.

Beaudricourt Yes, they must have been a comfort. Something not-human, holding all the truths, looking away. (*Pause.*) That contains deeds even such as mine, knows them and is pitiless and merciful all at once.

Gwynn Yes it was a beautiful idea.

Pause.

You know, what you did is . . . not – unique.

Beaudricourt No? To kill. To kill love. Not unique, *vraiment*.

Gwynn I tried to kill my husband.

Beaudricourt You joke with me.

Gwynn No, no joke.

Beaudricourt Tell me. I would be grateful if you could.

Pause.

Gwynn It was a Sunday – the boys had been packed off because we weren't civil even – poor lamb, he would drink and I put it back a bit too. You drank?

Beaudricourt I drank.

Gwynn We were a bit isolated, up the coast. I was trying to get my PhD done, not sleeping, working all hours – he was between jobs. And he was always taking the piss out of me doing what I was doing: yuppie, dyke, traitor, names, every day, names – and that day he, deliberately, while I was on my PC, he deliberately took out the power for the whole house – out, gone, like that – and I lost my work. Crap old PC, crashed. Files of it erased. Chapters – gone! A year's work. I screamed at him, 'You fucking ignorant bastard, Glynn.' He laughed at me, 'Ignorant of your toss, and happy to be so,' stuff like that, I mean he found it hard, I know, but my work, Jesus, my new life, the pain that had gone into that and I went at him with a – dictionary – a glossary of literary terms, hardback, yeah, whacked him in the chops, he fell back, whacked him over the head, he stumbled, down the stairs, head bouncing on the stairs, again and again,

I just did it to stop him laughing and he did, he just –
lay there – out cold. Oh God, I can still see the poor sod.

Pause.

Beaudricourt He lived?

Gwynn Yeah, oh yeah. He was fine. Bit gorey, but basically OK.

Beaudricourt That is the kindness, then.

Gwynn Yes. And he was nice about it, which was – awful – you know, I think the sober light of justice will . . . exonerate you.

Silence.

Beaudricourt Thank you for . . . your parable.

Gwynn It's not exactly counselling.

Beaudricourt And your – kisses.

Gwynn St John's Ambulance taught me all I know.

Beaudricourt I don't understand you much of the time.

Gwynn I'm just talking, y'know, to talk.

Kate and Fulton return; Dale and Fergus follow.

Kate Michel. (*She runs over to him.*) Michel . . .

Gwynn Careful.

Beaudricourt *Oui, oui, ma petite, oui.*

Fergus Y'all right there?

Beaudricourt nods.

Fulton Get closer in to the heat – Michel.

Dale It's burning well.

Fergus Fortuitous, that fire.

Fulton My idea.

Fergus Smart.

Pause.

Kate Are you OK?

Beaudricourt *Ça marche.*

Dale Where d'you learn firecraft?

Fulton Cubs. I only got so far, though. Scouts I didn't stick at – I found it – abrasive.

Fergus All those injunctions against wanking. If there'd been a badge for that I'd been well away.

Weak laughter.

Kate He shouldn't be in those wet clothes – I'm sorry, Michel, you should, er – we could – (*She takes off his trousers.*)

Fulton 'Off, off, you leavings.'

Kate Yes very nice but perhaps you could supply some warmth as I . . .

He takes off his jumper. Kate her coat. Fergus, his T-shirt. They undress Beaudricourt; he resists.

Kate Just allow us – please.

They dress him in their clothes.

Dale OK, who's got the harmonica?

Fergus Not 'Cum by Yar' now, is it? (*He giggles.*)

Gwynn Used to sing that with the Brownies.

Fergus You're a bit advanced for that –

Gwynn I was Brown Owl.

Fergus No way –

Gwynn Oh yes.

Fulton Father felt I should join the local pack to compensate for my isolation from the local community.

Dale Were you popular?

Fulton Popular? Even Akela despised me.

Silence.

Beaudricourt I don't know how to talk to you.

Kate You don't have to.

Beaudricourt Yes, I must – *il faut*. I must talk of this again and again.

Kate Don't –

Beaudricourt I can imagine how it will be – scandal, now. Vilification. Letters of support from colleagues. Angry editorials on lack of parity in law. Oh, worse – unsigned accounts of our unhappiness; of Marie's 'dogmatism', 'puritanical rectitude' etc. Friends, lovers will be drawn in. (*He looks at Kate.*)

Kate I'm equal to it.

Beaudricourt Then – a small sentence merely to humiliate; then permission to die – quietly. Whereas I wish to die now.

Kate It's better to live. On balance.

Beaudricourt The waves didn't let me drown. My body refused to stop floating. My mouth to swallow water.

Laughs, coughs, laughs. They join in. They stop.

Fergus What was that about?

Beaudricourt Like some book by Sartre. 'The Absurd.' (*He laughs.*)

Kate Ah, Sartre. Who reads him these days?

Beaudricourt Yes. He did some things – he said some – yes . . .

Sandy enters.

Sandy You're all together. Ah, a fire.

Fergus Beach party.

Dale This is not a beach.

Gwynn Beach party! (*Gwynn laughs.*)

Sandy Am I invited to this . . . party?

Gwynn I dunno. Is she invited?

Fergus Everyone nice is invited.

Gwynn There you are then.

Beaudricourt slowly stands, helped by Kate and Fulton.

Kate I've got him – thank you.

Fulton I was just – helping.

Beaudricourt Yes. Time. I must – go back. To her.

Kate Yes, yes, *nous rentrons*.

Beaudricourt Oui. *Et puis?*

Kate Oh. Sufficient unto the day.

Beaudricourt *Quoi?*

Kate Just, just take one step at a time.

They go slowly.

Fergus I'm cold.

Sandy You look really quite strange.

Dale Naked apostles.